500+ TIME-SAVING HINTS for EVERY WOMAN

Emilie Barnes

HARVEST HOUSE PUBLISHERS

EUGENE, OREGON

Cover by Terry Dugan Design, Minneapolis, Minnesota

Cover photos © Alex Wilson / Digital Vision / Getty Images; John Foxx / Alamy; Comstock Images / Alamy; Stockbyte Platinum / Alamy

Harvest House Publishers has made every effort to trace the ownership of all quotes. In the event of a question arising from the use of a quote, we regret any error made and will be pleased to make the necessary correction in future editions of this book.

500 TIME-SAVING HINTS FOR EVERY WOMAN
Copyright © 2006 by Emilie Barnes
Published by Harvest House Publishers
Eugene, Oregon 97402
www.harvesthousepublishers.com

Library of Congress Cataloging-in-Publication Data
Barnes, Emilie.
    500 time-saving hints for every woman / Emilie Barnes.
        p. cm.
    ISBN-13: 978-0-7369-1846-6 (pbk.)
    ISBN-10: 0-7369-1846-9 (pbk.)
    Product # 6918466
    1. Home economics. 2. Women—Time management. 3. Christian life. I. Title: Five hundred time-saving hints for every woman. II. Title.
    TX147.B25 2006
    640—dc22   2006002013

Printed in the United States of America

06   07   08   09   10   11   12   13   14   /   BP-MS   /   10   9   8   7   6   5   4   3   2   1

For 23 years readers have encouraged me with their notes and comments. Whether they speak with me at a conference or send me a letter or an email, the message has always been clear. "Thank you for teaching me the basics of managing a home. Your books have been like a second mother to me." This book is dedicated to you—my readers. Thank you for inspiring me.

Emilie Barnes

Contents

Section Five
Family Time

Section Six
Travel

Ready, Set, Organize!

To cover all the skills necessary to run a well-ordered home would take more pages than I'm allotted for one book. However, with the use of lists, quick ideas, and practical examples, this gathering of my favorite time-saving hints do cover the basic fundamentals of home management and simplified living. For easy reading and quick reference, I've limited the territory of this book to six areas:

- organization
- cleaning
- storage
- finance
- family time
- travel

At the end of the chapters, I have a section entitled "Simple Ideas." These extra thoughts, hints, and tips will make your life easier—I know this because these are ideas I use in my life.

I have watched countless women embrace a simpler, more efficient home-management style. It is amazing how adopting even a few changes each year can give you and your family much more time to enjoy your home, time with one another, and each day's blessings. I hope you will discover hints that suit your needs and that bring freedom and flexibility to your life. Enjoy.

SECTION ONE

Organization

Watch the path of your feet and
all your ways will be established.

PROVERBS 4:26 NASB

1

Setting Up Routines

Life is simpler when you have a routine and a certain rhythm. Imagine if a gymnast did not have a sense of rhythm or timing. There would be a lot of falling, tripping, and accidental tumbling. A routine would become complicated. The same thing happens to our daily routine when we do not consider the value of well-timed activities, planning, and simplified steps.

I have discovered that when I divide my days and weeks into segments and then plan, the scheduling is easier. You won't find a magic solution to maintaining a clean, well-organized home. Each individual and each family is different. If you create a routine that works for your lifestyle and cleanliness requirements, you can stay on top of your home. When you do plan and have a schedule, chores don't get out of hand.

> Since habits become power, make them
> work with you and not against you.
>
> E. STANLEY JONES

If you keep your home reasonably de-cluttered, clean, and neat, you'll avoid the need of marathon cleaning sessions. Depending on your lifestyle, you may find it easier to perform basic chores on a daily basis and relegate big chores to a weekend schedule. If you are one who likes to enjoy recreation on the weekends, you might want to tackle one room or one big chore every day, in addition to the daily chores, to allow time for leisure on the weekends.

I like to start out each week with things in order. Don't be surprised or disappointed when you have to continually be on top of the home. Disorganization will occur naturally. That's why a little each day—a routine—will prevent you from being overwhelmed. Also, remember Mom doesn't have to do it all. Proverbs 22:6 states: "Train up a child in the way he should go, and when he is old he will not depart from it" (RSV). Remember, if you are going to raise responsible children, you have to give them responsibility.

Each family will determine what level of neatness they expect. Some things, such as a clean kitchen and bathroom, are not negotiable—they are to be clean, but shelves or door moldings that don't pass the test may be acceptable. Keeping public rooms neat may be important to you, while other areas can occasionally slide.

May I stress that the master bedroom needs special attention? This area needs to be preserved for sleeping and romance. Often couples make this room a catchall—but this room is meant to be a sanctuary. Keep it neat and pretty. Be sure that the beds are made up immediately after the last person has gotten out of bed.

Here are basic tips to start a new cleaning routine in your home.

- Refrain from dumping and piling. Your home will feel more orderly and function better if at least the living and dining room aren't cluttered.

- Never pile up mail or projects on the dining room table, entry table, or coffee table.

- Before going to bed each night, have all the clutter picked up. Teach the children to put away their toys. Practice it every day.

- You'll be amazed at how much cleaning you can do in 15 minutes. Set a timer to see what can be accomplished in this little amount of time.

- I have found that an ostrich feather duster is the best dusting tool you can own. Their feathers have little vacuum-like ends that seem to suck up dust. They also can be cleaned easily in a mild detergent and warm water. Just hang to air dry.

- You can do minor chores while talking on a telephone. Remember, women can do more than one thing at a time. You can:
  o sweep the kitchen floor
  o wash a load of laundry
  o fold a load of wash
  o iron a few items of clothing
  o spray and wipe countertops, range top
  o scrub sink
  o wipe down refrigerator door
  o unload the dishwasher

It only takes 15 minutes a day and you'll be on your way to becoming a creative home organizer.

SIMPLE IDEAS

- Getting organized is not an end in itself. There is no right way to do things—it's got to be right for you.

- Order and organization is a way for us to function effectively.

- I have found that my motto "Do the Worst First" helps me get started. Once the worst is done, everything else is much easier.

- It takes 21 consecutive days of doing a new task before it becomes a habit.

2

Being Effective with Your Work

The busy person's greatest need is for "effective," not "efficient," planning. Being effective means choosing the right task from all the alternatives. Being efficient means doing any job that happens to be around. Planning is important because it saves you time in the end. Know what you have to do, and have your priorities established.

Often women will ask me, "How do you get more hours in your day?" Everyone is looking for a little magical pill that gives them more of that vital commodity called *time*. I really can't give you one simple trick that makes it all better; however, I've found that if you can eliminate long searches for whatever you're looking for, it will help you save time.

> Great men [women] never complain about the lack of time. Alexander the Great and John Wesley accomplished everything they did in twenty-four-hour days.
>
> FRED SMITH

I recently had a young woman call me on the phone. She was on the verge of tears as she said, "Every time I get the house organized and straightened up, it only takes a few days to get messed up again. What can I do? I'm so discouraged." No wonder she was upset. This young woman had a false understanding of organization. She assumed that once the house was organized, it should remain organized. I assured her that what she was experiencing was normal, and I told her not to be so disappointed when order returned to disarray. This is exactly what happens and exactly why it makes sense to manage the organization simply, effectively, and in a manner that suits how you and your family live.

Group Together Your Shopping Trips

With the high price of gasoline, we need to be wise shoppers and make good use of every trip. With a little bit of practice you can plan your shopping route to conserve the most gasoline and the most time. We waste so much time by getting in the car several times a day flitting to the market, then to the cleaners, then to the pharmacy, then to the children's activities, etc. Learn to get everything done with one trip.

In a notebook, keep a list of items you need to buy: books, videos, Christmas gifts, clothes, housewares, birthday and anniversary gifts. When you see a sale or go to an outlet store, you can purchase what's on your master list. This will save time and money in the long run.

Purchase More Than One Like Item

If you have frequent demands for like items—toiletries, pens, rulers, tape, scissors—store several of each item in strategic spots around the home. Don't waste time running all over the house to find a basic item. I started this when we had a two-story home. Having an extra vacuum cleaner and cleaning items upstairs was a time-saver.

Cut Short Unwanted Calls

When unwanted or unsolicited phone calls interrupt your day, they can really eat up a lot of valuable time. Learn to pay attention to caller ID and decide whether to answer. If you do answer and it is a sales call, keep in mind that it is not wise to purchase anything over the phone unless you know the person, and it is never okay to provide personal information. If you stand by these rules, there will not be any reason for you to linger over these unwanted calls or feel bad about making the conversation quick.

Organize to Save Time

My Bob used to waste time looking for the car keys and his glasses. One day I put up a decorative key hook by the phone in the kitchen and told him to put his car keys on the hook and to place his glasses on the counter underneath the keys. Done deal—no more problems.

Much of our disorganization is due to not having a place for everything, so we just lay it down. Soon we have clutter everywhere. I guarantee that if the following two mottoes are applied to how you process items, materials, papers, or even toys, you will be well on your way to a new and improved life of efficiency:

- Don't pile it. File it.
- Don't put it down. Put it away.

These two principles are lifesavers. Your clutter will disappear if you apply them for 21 days.

Do More Than One Thing at a Time

Even though women can naturally do more than one thing at a time, we still have to practice, practice, practice. Today's demanding lifestyle requires that we embrace the concept of multitasking. I personally can do any number of things while talking to a friend on the phone. I find that a cordless phone or cell phone gives me flexibility around the home. I have a "to read" folder I take with me when I know I'm going to have to wait for an extended time period. I also like to get caught up with all my junk mail, letters, and correspondence while waiting.

If you're into exercise and have an indoor exercise machine, this is a great time to read your favorite magazine or read your favorite new book while you work out. I personally find this a time where I can pray, meditate on Scripture, or even have some good background music playing.

> Some succeed because they are
> destined to, but most succeed
> because they are determined to.
>
> HENRY VAN DYKE

Determine Your Priorities

This is where my to-do list really comes in handy. Each evening before going to bed or before leaving the office at the end of the day, you can make a list of what you need to do tomorrow, and then go one step further by ranking your items according to priority. The next morning start working with number one, then go to number two. It's not long before you'll make a real impact on the list.

Use Your Body Clock

Each of us operates most efficiently at a certain time of day. Schedule taxing chores for the hours when your mind is sharpest. Do these chores when you have the most energy. This principle is not only good for home, but also at work if we work outside the home. Many women today have to be responsible for both areas.

Today's society has changed drastically since I was a young wife and mother. Roles for men and women and husbands and wives are quite different. Each family must work out their own division of labor. What works for one family may not be right for another family.

Track a 24-hour period and determine what part of the day is best for you. However, do not use this awareness as an excuse of not performing well in your off-period of the day. Many of us have to function at peak performance levels throughout the day.

Take Advantage of Delivery Services

Some areas of our society are returning back to the good old days when customer service was supreme. More and more companies are offering pick-up-and-delivery services. They are a valuable time-saver, and in most situations they are cost efficient. There are service companies that will also do this for you. This has become a home business opportunity. Traveling Nannies is a great business that employs men and women who are willing to run your errands. Consider finding this or a similar business in your town.

A high school or college student can run errands for you and your family. Many of our neighbors use such services. Our granddaughter, Christine, was such a nanny for a family this summer during her college break. She did everything. No two days were the same.

Many of us think only in terms of restaurants delivering their goods, but that kind of service has extended to most any category—local cleaners, grocers, personal shoppers, and many others.

Divide Big Jobs into Fast Tasks

I recommend you not look at the big tasks ahead of you. You will become overwhelmed and easily discouraged. It is better to learn how to break the whole into smaller parts which become fast tasks. These are little pieces you can readily handle. And step-by-step, you'll get the job done. Any of your tasks can be broken into small parts. The whole doesn't have to be accomplished in one sitting. Some might take you more than several days.

A good example might be when you want to reorganize the refrigerator. Set a time and work for 15 minutes. Work as fast as you can and get as much done as you can in that allotted time. If you didn't finish all you wanted to, tomorrow is another day and another 15 minutes. The same is true for cleaning out a cupboard or cleaning out the hall closet. Putting in a little bit of effort each day is better than not even attempting the project because it looks too big. You can always manage the fast tasks when you are overwhelmed with the whole.

Become a List Maker

In my daily planner, I have a list for almost everything. I write down everything from what to buy at Home Depot to a list of ingredients I need for a cooking project to good quotes I find for future books. Over the last few years I have kept a list of the medications I'm taking. This comes in so handy. Every new doctor wants to know what medications I am on.

Why waste time recreating this list? I find that list makers accomplish a lot more than non-list makers.

Start Using a Daily Planner

Stop looking for your checkbook, list of appointments, addresses, and telephone numbers. Put them all in your daily planner. There are many planners on the market today. If you are just starting out, I recommend you select one with a basic format. Some of the complicated systems can overwhelm and require too much tracking of details. You can always advance to more intricate planners as you grow accustomed to having a system.

Why a planner? Because we all realize we can't keep all the dates, facts, and information in our brain. The daily planner soon becomes your lifeline. Be sure your name, address, and phone numbers are written somewhere in your planner in case you should ever leave it or drop it while running errands.

Prevent Interruptions

Most people are interrupted at least once every five minutes. If this is true for you, then analyze your thieves of time at home as well as at work. When you study your time thieves, you will be amazed at how much time is lost by interruptions that could be avoided.

There is nothing wrong with telling people that you can see or talk to them at 9:30, 12:15, or 3:45. Even family members can be taught not to interrupt. Susanna Wesley's children knew that if she had her prayer apron over her head she wasn't to be interrupted. A dear friend of mine tells everyone not to call her on Wednesday. That's when she studies and prays. Her phone is never answered, but people can leave a message. I love to group my questions together so that when I call a person or company I have them written down. This saves my time and their patience!

When working at home, you can always signal to your family that you are not to be disturbed by closing your office door. The children need to know that emergencies always take precedence over these times. Don't prolong these closed door hours—or your family will stop respecting them.

Be a person who takes control of your time—don't let time control you. With a little study and observation, you can turn those "time interrupters" into "time-savers."

Quit Expecting Perfection

Perfectionism delays work from being accomplished. It's nice to want things done right, but not if you are crippled by inactivity. When you open your house to guests, you may know all the special extra touches you wanted to add, but your friends and guests won't know the difference. And just think how much lower your stress level will be if you let yourself enjoy activities and events without worrying about achieving perfection.

Enjoy the blessings of the day, if God sends them, and the evils of it bear patiently and sweetly; for this day only is ours, we are dead to yesterday, and we are not yet born to the morrow.

JEREMY TAYLOR

SIMPLE IDEAS

- Exercise while praying or watching TV. Learn to do more than one thing at a time.

- Whenever you catch yourself thinking, *I can do it later,* stop and make a point of doing it now.

- Make plans that require you to complete your chores by a certain date or time. This will put you into action.

- Ask yourself this question: "Is there an easier and better way to do this?"

- Don't wait until you have time to finish the entire task. Do as much as you can whenever you can.

- Don't interrupt yourself by starting another task before you've completed the first task.

- Do errands on the way to and from work.

- Learn to say no.

- Don't let work pile up. Decide which projects need to be completed and complete them.

- Keep in mind that there's no time like the present.

3

De-Cluttering Your Life

If you scratch your head and wonder why you are so disorganized, I can tell you why: The cause for disorganization is clutter. We stumble around looking for something because we have too much stuff in the way. Do you have piles and piles of clutter that get in your way? Oh yes, I know all of it is so important because someday you are going to need it. You give excuses like:

- It's a great conversation piece.
- The neighbors may want to borrow them someday.
- Maybe when my daughter gets this size, she can wear it.
- It may come in handy someday.
- I'm saving it for spare parts.
- Someday you won't be able to buy one of these.

All these excuses sound reasonable to you, but that reasoning will eventually cause you much wasted time and a great amount of stress. One of our favorite mottoes is: Less is best. When you're young you are a collector, and when you get older you begin to give things away. Don't wait until you're old to begin to reduce the clutter.

It doesn't have to be done overnight, but plant the seed in your mind that you are going to get rid of all the things you are hanging on to. There is real wisdom in letting go of things you no longer need or use. Change is a wonderful thing in life. That's one advantage of periodically moving—you have to get rid of a lot of items not worth relocating. Change allows you to pare away what you do not need. You can establish new priorities. Change and growth are both very stimulating to your well-being.

At my stage in life, my Bob and I have told our family and friends loud and clear, "We don't want any gift that can't be consumed or anything that takes up counter space or has to be polished, washed, or stored. We're glad to accept gift certificates for food, dinner out, a basket full of nuts, fruit, and vegetables, even a cruise to a romantic location will be appreciated, but please no stuff"

If you run out of time each day and cry out, "I need more hours in my day," you are probably working and stepping around too many piles, stacks, and things. Clutter makes every job take longer. The more you have, the more you have to work around. Trim down your stuff, and you will be amazed at how much more time you have in your day.

> Time is part of your life.
>
> DON ASLETT, CLEANING EXPERT

Just examine why it takes you so long to clean out your kitchen cupboard—too many dishes. Why you take so long to rearrange your walk-in closets—too many clothes and shoes. Why your drawers take so long to rearrange—too many socks, T-shirts, and underwear. Why rearranging the pantry closet takes so long—too many food items you don't need or use. A half hour here and a half hour there add up to a lost week every year. This lost time could be better used by reading, listening to music, going to the theater, taking a vacation, and enjoying your family.

Whenever we try to cram too much into a home, we pay a dear price by having to take care of all our possessions. This extra effort takes away from what we would really like to do. In Southern California where we live, one of the booming businesses is the building of storage units. Who do you think is their biggest customer base? Yes, people who store all their leftover junk. We know of people who spend $80 to $300 per month for someone else to store their clutter. Clutter and stuff cost a lot of money (and as Yogi Berra says, "Money is just like cash").

I can remember when garages were for parking cars. Now the cars are parked outside in the inclement weather while we use our garages for extra storage space. We have neighbors whose garages look like sporting goods stores. Every imaginable piece of equipment is either on the floor, hanging on the walls, or tucked into a plastic bin stored on a rack.

Medical doctors will tell you that many of the illnesses in America are mentally or emotionally induced. Much of this illness is caused by people who are stressed-out looking after all their junk. We spend so much time, energy, and money worrying about our stuff that we weaken our immune systems. And when our body's defense system is down, we are more vulnerable to attracting a disease or illness. For your health's sake, clear out that clutter. Out of sight is out of mind.

Ways to de-clutter:

- *Rent, don't buy.* An item that you don't use very often shouldn't be bought and then stored. Not only do you save money, but you don't have to lug, store, and insure it.

- *It's what we have too much of, not too little of, that causes us problems.* Just think about this! Have you ever had a problem over something you don't have? Here is a perfect example: If you have a boat, you have boat problems. Someone once said BOAT stands for Bring On Another Thousand. Since Bob and I don't own a boat, we don't have boat problems. If we want a day in a boat, we go rent one. When we return it, the man in charge asks, "Did you have a good time?" And we say, "Yes, we did!" We leave him to clean the boat, clean the cabin, dock the boat, pay the slip fee, pay the insurance, and make all the repairs. What a deal.

- *Don't rent a storage unit.* The only reasons a storage unit might make sense is to store past records for the Internal Revenue Service or for the short-term storage of furniture or packed boxes during a relocation. Otherwise, storage units are just places you store things you no longer use. And they are an expensive way to delay throwing out such items.

- *Have a garage sale and get rid of all the unused items.* Why pay the eventual extra cost of moving items you never use? Get rid of them now.

- *Make the decision to de-clutter.* You must make up your mind that you are going to get rid of all the clutter in your life. It might be at home or in the office. If you don't plan to plan you will never do—and you will spend all your life working around those things that distance you from what you truly want to be doing.

SIMPLE IDEAS

- In order to have order, you must figure out what your goals and purposes are in life.

- People don't plan to be failures, but they do plan if they are going to be successful.

- A goal is nothing but a dream with a deadline. Set the goal and the deadline.

- On paper, list ten goals you wish to reach by the end of the year, and then do them.

- The key to organization is to start now—no matter what. If you have a call to make, start dialing.

- Five-minute pick-up: Pick up your feather duster and dust each room for five minutes. Time yourself with the kitchen timer.

- It's not what you get that makes you successful; it is what you do with what you've got.

- Think of clutter as a poor investment. It robs us of valuable time we could spend doing important and fulfilling things.

4

Trading Procrastination for Preparation

Planning is crucial if we are going to realize our purpose in life. Women gain a feeling of security when they have a firm feeling of what the future holds. We love planning and love husbands who also feel compelled to plan for tomorrow. This concept of being prepared gives us a great deal of satisfaction and confidence.

Couples who can plan together are more likely to succeed in life than the non-planners. Yes, it does take more time to plan than not to plan, but in the long run it is so beneficial for the family.

A house painter can tell you that the most important part of his job is the preparation process. Not only does the preparation lead to a faster, cleaner project, it also ensures lasting value of the paint job. How one prepares for life will play a large part in determining how successful life will be.

Another of our favorite mottoes is: The wise woman does in her youth what the foolish woman does in her old age. Start planning when you're young and don't wait until you get old.

> For which one of you, when he wants
> to build a tower, does not first sit down
> and calculate the cost to see if he has
> enough to complete it? Otherwise, when
> he has laid a foundation and is not able
> to finish, all who observe it begin to
> ridicule him, saying, "This man began
> to build and was not able to finish."
>
> LUKE 14:28-30 NASB

The Power of Procrastination

Many people are paralyzed because of their inability to make a decision and get their gearshift into drive. One of the ways we are ineffective in our lives is by the evil time-waster called *procrastination*.

In adults, procrastination generally signals some kind of internal conflict. After we have made the decision to do something, a part of us still holds us back. Why?

- We feel overwhelmed.
- We overestimate the amount of time needed.
- We would rather be doing something else.
- We think if we wait long enough, the task will go away.
- We fear failure.
- We fear success.
- We are used to a state of panic.

The idea that procrastinators are simply lazy is a myth, and their behavior rarely is changed by just deciding to stop procrastinating. Those who put off something do so because of some form of fear. Here are just a few of those fears:

- They're so afraid of failure that they would rather not try than try and fail.
- They're afraid that their success could distance people from them.

- They feel that they must be in control of their life—procrastination allows a sense (although a false sense) that they are in control.

- They are afraid of creating or accomplishing something on time because they have always relied on the adrenalin rush that comes with doing things last minute.

These fears might keep many folks from looking for a solution to their procrastination problems. But if you are ready to trade this destructive habit for the helpful practice of preparation, then here are 14 ways to make a change.

1. Make yourself a "Call, Do, See" list. Use the last five to seven minutes of each day to jot down several activities that need to be done tomorrow.

2. Keep a log of how long various projects take (usually shorter than you thought).

3. Work with the time available to you, breaking the task into small bites.

4. Make time by saying no to lesser projects and blocks of time.

5. Do things as they come to you.

6. Eliminate distractions.

7. Make it easy to work by grouping like things or activities together.

8. Reward yourself for getting started.

9. Tell someone else what your deadline is.

10. Expect problems. Things don't always go as expected.

11. Learn to delegate.

12. Start today. Don't wait for tomorrow!

13. Start with small tasks first.

14. Be patient and don't expect change overnight. Remember, it takes 21 days to form a new habit.

With your computer and printer you can design your own to-do list. If you don't have this technology, you can very simply take a sheet of paper and write at the top of the page:

Call: **Do:**   **See:**

Some people like to create a fresh list every day. Others prefer to have one ongoing for the week. I highly recommend that you start this practice if you do not use some form of list currently. Even if you find it difficult to refer back to your list throughout the day, putting thoughts, goals, and tasks in writing helps you achieve them. Pretty soon, procrastination will become unappealing and will seem like the long way and wrong way to get something done.

SIMPLE IDEAS

- A sense of direction and a plan can make the difference between responsible family living and just surviving.

- God delights in turning weakness into strength and transforming chaos into order.

- Give one item away every day.

- Remember that by using small bits of time faithfully, you can accomplish great things.

- Finish tasks. Complete one project before you start another.

- Reward yourself for a job well done. Keep it healthy.

- Time management is not just keeping busy; it is finding God's focus for you.

- An organized life will give you more time to do things that are more valuable.

- We can make our plans, but the final outcome is in God's hands. —Proverbs 16:1 TLB

- The time to relax is when you don't have time for it. —Sydney J. Harris

5

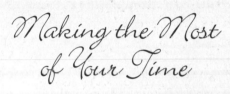

*Making the Most
of Your Time*

Do you consider your time to be a premium commodity? I have had women tell me over and over how much they appreciate even a few extra minutes. Juggling a husband, children, a home, and maybe a home business can test even the most organized. Those who are organized still end up with gaps in their day. An event starts later than planned. A child is late coming home from basketball practice. A work meeting is delayed.

Recently I decided to try and estimate how many minutes the average person wasted or lost each day. I came up with approximately two and a half hours—in just one day! Now if we had that two and a half hours all in a single block of time, we could accomplish a great deal. But in five-minute segments, not much can get done. Or can it? Think of some small jobs that can be accomplished in very limited amounts of time. You'll be surprised by the short amount of time it takes to do many jobs.

I, Wisdom, will make the hours of
your day more profitable and the
years of your life more fruitful.

PROVERBS 9:11 TLB

31

Do you ever find yourself with nothing to do, maybe while at the bank standing in a slow-moving line, at the doctor's office waiting for a doctor who isn't on time, at the Department of Motor Vehicles hoping they'll call your name or number. Well, I have been there, and I've discovered a solution: The Five-Minute File. The plan provides you with a convenient way to accomplish tasks you are unable to do while at home, at the office, or while running errands. I utilize this concept to eliminate small tasks that can otherwise become overwhelming. So what exactly is a Five-Minute File? It's really quite simple.

What You Will Need

- Two sturdy pocket-type file folders (these work best because they keep small papers and notes from falling out).
- Stenographer's pad or a computer-generated form.
- A timer, preferably one that allows you to set more than one time allotment at a time.

What You Do

- Sit down with a cup of tea or coffee and begin making a list of chores and small tasks that can be completed in five minutes or less. Every woman's list will differ, but the concept is the same.
- Make a simple chart on your computer or your pad of paper. Include space to check off tasks you have completed. Some of the items, such as sweeping the front sidewalk, washing out the kitchen trash can, tightening the loose screw in the back gate, sweeping out the garage, vacuuming the inside of the car, etc., will be one-time deals. Other tasks are ongoing, like cleaning and organizing.
- You will add and delete items regularly, so keep the folder handy.
- In one of the file folders, store articles and mail to be read. You

can grab it on your way out the door. In the other folder, keep your list.

This is a sample of tasks that might be on your Five-Minute File list. I imagine this list will inspire you to think of many other quick duties or chores.

- Pick some flowers from the garden and arrange them in a vase.
- Unload the dishwasher.
- Order items over the telephone or on the computer.
- Write a thank-you note.
- Go through the mail, filing in appropriate family members' color-coded folders. Place items to read later in your Five-Minute File.
- Feed and water the animals.
- Refill the business card holder.
- Refill paper in the printer.
- Work on your to-do list for the next day.
- Make calls to confirm any meetings for the next day.

Use the Five-Minute File any time you have a few spare minutes. Make the file a family activity. Next time your child is waiting for a ride, hand them the file and let them choose a task they can complete in five minutes or less. They will be contributing to the family as a whole and utilizing their time responsibly.

The main reason we don't get more accomplished is because we lack an organized way to determine what needs to be done. By writing down projects and keeping them in a simple file, you will automatically be organizing yourself and your family.

There is nothing more rewarding than getting tasks completed in a timely manner. Take your planner and your lists with you whenever you go out on errands. You may be able to fit in something you scheduled for later in the week.

Fast Prioritizing

Does your to-do list seem out of control or filled with such important things that you could not possibly delete one of them? Well, I have some good news for you. The 80/20 rule is one of the greatest principles you can use to determine your top priorities. If all of the items on your to-do list are arranged in order of value, 80 percent of the value would come from only 20 percent of the items. The remaining 20 percent of the value would come from 80 percent of the items. Sometimes a little more and sometimes a little less.

So look at a list of ten tasks—doing the first two of them will yield 80 percent of the value. Don't be overwhelmed by a large list. Remember, the top 20 percent of the list gives 80 percent of the value. What's left undone today can go on the list for tomorrow.

These examples help you visualize the importance of concentrating on high-value tasks:

- 80 percent of sales come from 20 percent of customers
- 80 percent of production is in 20 percent of the product line
- 80 percent of sick leave is taken by 20 percent of employees
- 80 percent of file usage is in 20 percent of files
- 80 percent of dinners repeat 20 percent of recipes
- 80 percent of dirt is on 20 percent of floor areas that are highly used
- 80 percent of eating out is done at 20 percent of favorite restaurants
- 80 percent of volunteer hours are contributed by 20 percent of the volunteers
- 80 percent of a church's budget is given by 20 percent of the membership

Everything should be done in
a fitting and orderly way.

1 CORINTHIANS 14:40

Create a Map of Your Time

In all of my previous organizational books (see www.emiliebarnes. com) I have recommended using a large desktop calendar. In fact the bigger the better. And purchase a calendar that has very large squares.

As soon as you receive invitations, announcements, school events, church activities, etc., simply transfer the important data onto the appropriate square of your large calendar. Then take the cards or fliers and paper clip them to the back of the month in which the event takes place. If the square is large enough to write down all the info, you can toss that unwanted piece of paper. Trying to keep up with all these pieces of paper can be mind-boggling, to say the least.

Having control over your life can give one a tremendous feeling of freedom. A big calendar will help you accomplish this goal. For once you will have all your scheduled events recorded in one place. I write down dental and doctor appointments and upcoming service on the automobiles. I also add birthday dates and wedding anniversaries in the squares. This way I don't miss a favorite friend's celebration. At the beginning of each year, I just transfer all the important dates to my new calendar. Does it take time to do this? Yes, but a lot less time than tracking down someone's birthday or an anniversary date.

At the end of each year I file these calendars. They become a historical record of family events for that year. This kind of record keeping helps you recall all your adventures when you sit down and write that all-important Christmas letter.

SIMPLE IDEAS

- Remember, your goal is to get organized so that you can work toward your purpose in life.

- Practice the 45/15 rule. After every 45 minutes of focused work, take a 15-minute break. Go for a short walk or do some stretching exercises. Do one of the tasks in your Five-Minute File.

- Color code your file folders. The red folders can be hot items. Use bright colors—they are more cheerful.

- Keep a pad of paper and pen next to your bed to jot down ideas that come to you at night.

- When you order entertainment or travel tickets in advance, file them in envelopes in a logical place. Replacement can be difficult and costly to obtain at the last minute.

- Save appliance manuals and warranty information in one place (either in a file folder or use a three-ring binder). Record serial numbers and model numbers on each manual. Attach the original receipt for future reference.

- Remind yourself of important items with Post-it Notes on your bathroom mirror or on the door you leave by in the mornings—anywhere to get your attention.

- Keep track of who borrowed books or kitchen items on index cards.

6

Paper, Paper, What Do You Do with All the Paper

∞

You can set your watch by the time of day our mailman brings the mail (2:05 PM) Monday through Saturday. I can't wait for the mail to arrive. With great anticipation I open the door to my large metal box and out tumbles junk mail, personal letters, unfortunate bills, and mail-order catalogs. As I go back into the house and sift through the pieces, I realize I must do something with all this paper.

The thought of processing numerous bills, solicitations, advertisements, and other pieces of unwanted mail can be depressing. What do I save? Where do I put the items we need to read? And what do I throw away?

Every day we all must make decisions about paper, and if we are to keep our sanity, we must stay on top of this mountain. It seems as though we must sort through large piles of paper that accumulate from day-to-day, week-to-week, and month-to-month. I hear of many stories from individuals about how all this paper has created a very large problem in their lives. One lady couldn't use her dining room table without a major paper transfer—which she only did once in a while when she entertained friends. Another woman's husband—fed up with piles stacked on counters, refrigerator, desk, game table, dressers, and even on the floor—threatened "Either the paper goes or I go." That ultimatum caused her to bring her paper problem under control. If you look around, many of our messes relate to not having a plan on how to handle paper.

In our home, my Bob opens and controls the mail flow. In your home, you may be the one doing this. When you go through the mail each day (I stress each day), the golden rule is: Work through today's mail before tomorrow's mail arrives. Have a recycle bin or a trash can nearby. Get in the habit of quickly deciding what goes in the trash. Don't hesitate to toss junk mail and unwanted catalogs. Don't be concerned about what you will be missing if you don't read or thumb through them. After all, the same junk mail will arrive again in a couple of weeks. If you can get in the habit of instantly tossing out junk mail, you will get rid of 30 to 50 percent of your daily mail.

Here are a few other time-savers for speeding up processing of the mail:

- For mail that requires input from another family member, I put a note or question mark on it so we can discuss it. Removable self-stick note pads are great for this.

- Often I don't have immediate time to read catalogs, publications, fliers, missionary letters, or letters of inquiry. I slip them into a file folder and take them with me when I run errands. When I have to wait in a doctor's office, for children getting out of an activity, a long line at the bank or post office, I use this time to catch up on my reading. As I read, I may make notes on it, and when I'm done I toss it or process it according to the subject matter.

- Address changes should be noted immediately upon receipt of notification; make sure to cross out the old. I recommend putting addresses in pencil. This makes changes a lot easier. If you use computer files, the change is even easier. However, whichever method you use, do it immediately.

- It seems as though everyone has a business card for themselves, a business, or a home business. What do you do with all these cards? Go to your stationery store and purchase a plastic business card holder that fits into your daily planner (cards you don't use regularly could go into the same kind of holder, but it would be stored in your desk area). The next time you get a business card, just file it away. If you won't be using that person's services, consider tossing that card.

- When the children were home, Bob would take their personal mail and place it on their beds. Another good method is to have a folder with each child's name on it and insert their mail into the appropriate file folder. Put it on a work desk, a kitchen table, or some common location where they could retrieve it when they arrive home from school.

Much of our unrest occurs when we don't make a routing decision the first time we touch the piece of paper. The more items we take care of with the first touch, the better the process becomes. It takes practice but it is possible. Unfortunately, most of us aren't there yet. Let's see how we can organize so we never have to be buried under the paper mountain again.

A. Schedule time to sort through papers. Put it on your daily schedule. If you don't schedule it you won't do it.

B. Gather some basic materials to help you get organized.

- Cardboard file boxes or an upright file cabinet.
- File folders. I like brightly colored folders, but plain manila will do.
- Plain white #10 envelopes
- Black felt-tip pens
- Black plastic trash bags—30-gallon size works great.

C. Start wherever the clutter annoys you most. Determine to work your way through every pile of paper. Go through your dresser drawers and closets wherever paper has accumulated. Continue to set times until the project is completed. Allot at least 15 minutes each day to this project.

D. Determine to throw away anything you don't need.

E. Develop a simple and thorough file system.

- Label brightly colored file folders with a medium-point pen.
- File categories might include:
  - IRS tax information per year
  - charge (credit cards) accounts
  - utility receipts
  - insurance policies
  - insurance claims
  - car repair receipts
  - Bible study notes and outlines
  - mortgage information
  - photos/negatives
  - travel information
  - warranties
  - vacation ideas
- Label a file folder for each member of the family. These files can be used to keep health records, report cards, notes, drawings, awards, and other special remembrances.
- Within each file, use plain 8 x 10 envelopes to separate accounts. For example, in the "Utility Receipts" folder, there might be separate envelopes labeled:
  - gas
  - oil
  - telephone
  - water
  - city
  - garbage/collection

- When necessary, add files so no one file is too thick. Instead of one insurance file, there might be separate folders for home, car, health, life, etc.
- Handle each piece of paper once if at all possible.

F. Store your files in an-out-of-sight place if at all possible. Be sure it is easily accessible. If a box contains crucial records that might need to be removed in an emergency, put a bright red dot on the box so it can be easily recognized.

Accordion files are wonderful in that they have many versatile uses—all the way from storing bills for future payment to storing important papers, greeting cards, and thank-you cards. You can set the files up with labels for each category. Here are some ideas.

- pay
- read
- answer
- pending
- hold
- correspondence
- a tickler file for each day

SIMPLE IDEAS

- In handling mail, buy flat baskets, wire bins, or wood boxes for "In" and "Out" boxes.
- Use a metal vertical sorter and file folders to sort bills. Set aside 30 minutes each week for personal paperwork, including children's schoolwork and reports.
- Buy a flat basket to organize newspapers for recycling. Designate a recycling spot.
- Save bank statements, credit card statements, receipts for purchase (in case of return), investment statements, utility statements, canceled

checks or copies, pay stubs, and family medical records, such as immunizations.

- Don't let anyone steal your Social Security, bank account, or credit card numbers. Invest in a wastebasket shredder. Separate the shreds when you throw them away.

- Computer manuals are most useful near the computer. Store master software disks (including compact discs) and registration numbers near your computer.

- Get rid of extra paper. Almost 90 percent of the paper in your home or office is never looked at again. Get rid of as much of it as possible.

- Providing secure protection for some of your records is important. You can use a waterproof, heat-resistant metal lockbox or a safe. Consider the safe-deposit box service at your bank.

- When you receive a magazine, quickly go through it and tear out the articles you find interesting. File them away in your Five-Minute File for later reading.

Today

This is the beginning of a new day.
God has given me this day to use as I will.
I can waste it or use it for good.
What I do today is important, because
I'm exchanging a day of my life for it.
When tomorrow comes,
this day will be gone forever,
leaving in its place something
that I have traded for it.
I want it to be gain, not loss;
good, not evil;
success, not failure;
in order that I shall not regret
the price I paid for it.
Yesterday is history,
tomorrow's a mystery
today is a gift,
that's why we call it the present.

AUTHOR UNKNOWN

Cleaning

Look at your home as an extension
of your personality and
the warmth of your being.

7

When and How to Clean

Women will often ask me, "How do you know what, when, and how often to clean?" It seems so elementary to me, but I forget that many women never had a mother who taught them to be a maker of a home. Cleaning a home, while necessary, is a very personal issue. Don't worry about other people's standards. Decide what clean means to you and keep house accordingly. To help you organize and develop a routine for cleaning, I suggest that you gather the following tools:

- Set up a 3 x 5 colored-card file box with dividers and tabs.
- Label dividers in this card file as follows:
  - Daily
  - Weekly

- Monthly
- Quarterly
- Semiannually
- Annually

Make a list of jobs that need to be done in each category and file behind each tab. For example:

1. Daily

- do dishes
- make beds
- clean bathrooms
- pick up rooms
- clean kitchen
- take out trash
- take care of any animals you have

2. Weekly

- Monday—wash, grocery shop
- Tuesday—iron, water plants
- Wednesday—mop floors
- Thursday—vacuum, go shopping
- Friday—change bed linens
- Saturday—do yard work, sweep front porch and entry
- Sunday—keep free for family activities such as church, picnic, beach, movie, etc.

Note: If you skip a job on the assigned day, don't do it the next day. Put the card at the back of the file section and wait until next week.

3. Monthly

- clean out refrigerator
- clean oven

- mend clothing
- clean and dust all baseboards
- sweep the garage
- vacuum furniture
- clean inside and outside of windows
- check filters on heating and cooling system and change as necessary

4. Quarterly

- clean drawers
- clean out bedroom dresser drawers
- clean china cabinets

5. Semiannually

- clean all house screens
- rearrange furniture, vacuum under all old placement

6. Annually

- wash down all walls
- check smoke detectors
- clean out garage
- touch up interior walls and door trim with paint
- make home repairs as they occur
- shampoo carpets if needed
- wash sheer curtains
- clean drapes throughout home

Feel free to add any other reminders you might want to go on your cards. It's amazing how much better our homes function when we maintain, organize, and clean them in a regular fashion. When you discover ways to help yourself, you will also discover that all these tasks are manageable.

> Just as Jesus found it necessary to
> sweep the money-changers from
> the temple porch, so we ourselves
> need a lot of house cleaning.
>
> DALE EVANS ROGERS

Surviving Stains

Stains, stains go away, don't come back any other day. I do whatever I can to prevent stains from appearing around our home. Over the years, I've tried every stain remover on the grocery shelves. Some work and others don't.

I've found that if I don't treat stains quickly, they set and become permanent. Take immediate action to stop a stain from spreading or sinking deeper into the surface of the fabric. Blot up the spill with a clean cloth, absorbing tissue, or salt.

Most stains fall into four categories:

1. Stains that can be removed with normal washing—water-based paints and milk.

2. Stains that can be removed by bleaching or the combination of a hot wash and detergent—tea, fruit juice, or nonpermanent ink pen.

3. Stains requiring a prewash treatment and/or soak before washing—grass stains or blood.

4. Stains requiring special treatment before cleaning—gloss paint.

Be sure to check a garment before attempting to remove a stain. Even though the label might read "colorfast," attempt to apply the cleaner on an out-of-sight part of the garment. If color seeps onto a clean cloth, the garment should be taken to the cleaners.

Specific carpet and upholstery foams and dry-cleaning fluids are available, but unless you are certain that you can deal with a stain successfully yourself, it is advisable to call in a professional cleaner.

Stain Removal Secrets

Stains can be one of the toughest obstacles to a clean home and to clean clothes. Any house with kids or pets or even adults is going to endure spills. Stains are most successfully removed if they are noticed and cleaned right away. There are some great products to have in the house that will aid in quick removal. Products you may already have on hand—hydrogen peroxide, borax, and white wine vinegar—are great for neutralizing many stains. Some less common solutions to add to your cleaning supply closet include denatured alcohol and paint thinner.

Many problem stains can be cleaned with simple steps.

- *Ballpoint pen*—Dab with nail polish remover or rubbing alcohol.

- *Blood*—Rinse off under cold running water and then soak in a solution of biological washing liquid. Soak white garments in a mild ammonia/water solution and then wash.

- *Burns*—Scorch marks can sometimes be rubbed off with a blunt knife. Treat fabric with a little diluted glycerine and wash as usual. Treat stubborn burns with a hydrogen peroxide solution of 1 part to 9 parts water.

- *Butter and margarine*—Scrape off as much of the grease as possible and then apply a biological liquid (enzymatic cleanser) to the area. Wash in as high a temperature as the fabric will stand.

- *Candle wax*—Carefully pick or scrape off the cooled wax using a blunt knife. Place paper towels above and beneath the soiled area, then iron over the top paper, replacing it as soon as it becomes saturated with wax. Repeat until no more wax comes off. With colored wax you may want to treat with denatured alcohol before washing. I have found that an ice cube rubbed over the candle wax hardens the wax and helps it come off the fabric easier.

- *Chewing gum*—Place the garment in the freezer and then pick off the solid matter. Dab with denatured alcohol or dry-cleaning fluid.

- *Chocolate*—Apply biological washing liquid to the stain. Sponge the area with warm water before washing as usual.

- *Coffee*—Wash immediately under cold-running water and then soak in a strong detergent solution. Treat stubborn marks with a hydrogen-peroxide solution (1 part hydrogen peroxide to 9 parts water) before washing.

- *Crayon*—Dab the soiled area with paint thinner. Use a heavy-duty detergent containing oxygen bleach for the remainder of the clean up.

- *Egg*—Scrape off the excess using a blunt knife and then wash with a biological washing liquid applied to the stain. Old stains can be removed by using the hydrogen-peroxide formula. Then wash as usual.

- *Fats, grease, and cooking oils*—Dampen the fabric with water and apply heavy-duty liquid detergent to the stain. Wash immediately in the hottest water the fabric will take.

- *Fruit and fruit juice*—Sprinkle borax over the stain to absorb the moisture and to neutralize the acid. Rinse in cold water before washing in a solution of hot water and detergent. Treat stubborn marks with a solution of diluted household bleach and water (1 part bleach to 4 parts water).

- *Grass stains*—Dab with denatured alcohol (not to be used on acetate or tri-acetate fabrics), rinse, and wash.

- *Heat rings*—Rub along the grain of the wood with a soft cloth dipped in turpentine. Alternatively, metal polish rubbed over the marks should remove them. Wipe surface with a clean, damp cloth before repolishing.

- *Inks*—Dab unknown inks with nail polish remover. Cover blue and black fountain pen ink with salt and lemon juice, and leave them overnight. Finally, rinse and wash with a biological liquid detergent.

- *Jam*—Scrape off the excess using a blunt knife and then dab with a prewash laundry aid. Wash as usual.

- *Tomato ketchup*—Scrape off the excess before holding under cold running water. Dab the area with a little biological washing liquid and then wash as usual. Treat deep stains with the hydrogen peroxide solution.

- *Lipstick*—Dab first with paint thinner and then apply a liquid detergent straight on the mark and work it into the fibers. Wash in water as hot as the fabric will stand.

- *Milk*—Rinse under cold running water and then wash using a biological detergent.

- *Nail polish*—Dab with nail polish remover or acetone before washing as usual. Noncolorfast fabrics should be dry-cleaned professionally.

- *Perspiration*—Dab with a solution of 1 part white wine vinegar to 10 parts water, or treat the affected area with biological prewash detergent and then wash as usual.

- *Shoe polish*—Dab the area either with a grease solvent or denatured alcohol. Soak in a strong detergent solution and then wash as usual.

- *Urine*—Soak in a gentle solution of cold water and ammonia. Alternatively, soak for a short time with biological washing liquid before washing in the hottest water the fabric will stand.

- *Vomit*—Scrape off the excess or blot it with old cloths. Scrub with a solution of warm water and a biological detergent to which a little white-wine vinegar and disinfectant have been added. Rinse and repeat if necessary before washing.

- *Wine*—For *red wine,* cover the stain with salt and then scrape up the saturated salt/wine mixture before blotting with clean, absorbent cloths. Apply cold water to the affected area. Always work from the outside in, to prevent the stain from spreading. Blot again and clean in the usual manner. For *white wine,* blot up as much as possible with a dry cloth. Treat with cold water before washing.

Stain Removal Tips

- Always follow the manufacturer's directions before using any stain remover products.
- Never mix chemicals—if you do, the resulting fumes could be lethal.
- Never smoke or have an exposed flame near cleaning fluids, as many are highly flammable.
- Keep the room well ventilated while working with cleaning fluids.
- Wear household gloves when using solvent and bleach cleaners.
- Consider hiring a professional when attempting to clean stains off of expensive carpets and upholstery.

SIMPLE IDEAS

- When using a sink full of hot water to rinse the dishes, add a capful of vinegar to cut any excess grease or soap. This will give your dishes a clean, sparkling look.
- To clean the inside of your washing machine and remove soap scum, run the machine through a rinse cycle with two cups of vinegar.
- To clean windows and mirrors with no streaks, wipe off cleaner with newspaper instead of paper towels.
- A good ceramic tile cleaner is a mixture of ¼ cup ammonia, ½ cup baking soda, and 1 gallon warm water.
- To prevent soap buildup in your soap dish, cut a sponge to fit the soap dish. After using the soap, place it on the sponge. This makes for easy cleaning later.
- To prevent the nozzle on a can of spray paint from becoming clogged, turn the can upside down after each use and depress the spray head until the air is clear of paint.

8

Keeping the Kitchen Healthy

Besides the time we spend sleeping and working, we spend the most time in the kitchen. While raising my family, I spent many, many hours in the kitchen. I found it to be a safe and pleasant sanctuary for me. I liked caring for my family, preparing meals, and spending personal time in the sunny room. It would never have occurred to me that this happy place was also the most germ-infested room in the house. It always looks clean! But when I was dealing with cancer, I attended disease control classes at the hospital and discovered how easy it was to be in contact with germs in the kitchen.

The good news is that you can safeguard your family by making sure that the food they eat is always safe. How you shop for, store, and handle food can have lasting effect on the health of your family. As the woman of the home, you must understand how germs breed and travel.

Easy Methods for a Safe Kitchen

These methods for keeping food and your food preparation area safe are simple, but they do require you to be diligent and conscientious. Once you put these steps into practice, they will become second nature and will save you time and energy. They will also save you some money on food—the better preserved food is, the longer it will last.

I encourage you to teach your other family members these ideas so that they become a standard in your home.

1. Watch the temperature of food. Keep chilled and frozen food cold between buying it and storing it at home. Food warms up while you transport it home; leaving chilled food in a shopping bag or car for any length of time can raise the temperature sufficiently to allow bacteria to grow and multiply. At home, transfer chilled or frozen food to the freezer or refrigerator immediately.

2. Periodically check the temperature in the freezer and refrigerator. Make sure the temperature is cold enough for the proper food storage. If it is not cold enough, harmful bacteria can grow and may cause food poisoning—anything from stomach upset to serious illness.

3. Store the most perishable food in the coldest part of the refrigerator. These are:

- precooked chilled foods
- soft cheeses
- cooked meats
- cream or custard filled cakes
- prepared salads
- potato salads
- desserts
- home-prepared food and leftovers

Food that must be kept cool can be stored in cool zones. These are:

- milk
- yogurt
- fruit juices
- low-fat spreads

- hard cheeses
- opened jars and bottles
- butter/margarine
- eggs

The salad crisper is the warmest part of the refrigerator. It is designed for storing whole vegetables, fruit, lettuce, tomatoes, radishes, etc. Try to keep raw meat, poultry, and fish on the bottom shelf in case they drip. I place these items on a plate so that if they do drip they won't mess up the refrigerator. Prevent meats from touching other meats or other foods by storing them in separate containers for added safety.

Look to your health; and if you
have it, praise God and value it
next to a good conscience.

IsAAk WALTON

4. Don't keep food too long and observe the "use by" dates. Once opened, canned food can be kept in the refrigerator up to 48 hours. (However, I always remove the unused food from the can and store in a plastic container.)

5. Avoid cross-contamination. Bacteria will easily cross from one food to another, especially from raw meat to cooked or processed foods, so the prevention of cross-contamination is very important for anyone in charge of preparing food for others. Be sure to wash your hands very carefully after handling raw chicken or other meat.

6. Keep insects out of your kitchen as much as possible. This sounds obvious, but in some parts of the country and in some climates bugs can be more of a problem than in others. Flies and cockroaches can transfer germs, so it is very important to keep them away from food. When selecting an insect-repellant, make sure there are no harmful chemicals used. Try to use herbal repellants as much as possible. Always cover food that is left out any period of time.

7. Take time to disinfect your garbage disposal. Often we never think about this piece of equipment being a germ carrier. However, this is where all the garbage is taken out of the kitchen. I disinfect the rubber ring around the opening of the disposal about every two weeks to prevent germs from building up and infesting surrounding food. While you're at it, you might consider putting some liquid drain cleaner down your kitchen sink drain. This helps dissolve grease that has a tendency to clog your drains and cause the kitchen and bathroom fixture to back up.

8. Cook food properly. High temperatures kill most bacteria, so always make sure that raw food, especially meat, is cooked as it should be. The center temperature should reach 158°F for at least two minutes. In large meat portions, make sure that the center is well-cooked; a good meat thermometer can help. Microwave cookers do not always heat food to the high temperatures that kill food-poisoning bacteria, so when using them, make sure the food is piping hot at the center before serving. When reheating food, always heat until it is hot all the way through. Never reheat food more than once.

If frozen meats are not completely thawed, the center may not be properly cooked. Raw eggs sometimes contain bacteria, which is destroyed by cooking. The current thinking is that you should not use recipes requiring uncooked eggs.

SIMPLE IDEAS

- Keep the coldest part of the refrigerator between 32 and 41°F.

- Wrap and cover all raw and uncooked foods.

- Return perishable foods—such as butter and mayonnaise—to the refrigerator as soon as possible after use.

- Don't overload the refrigerator; this can block the circulation of the cooling air.

- Don't put hot foods in the refrigerator; let them cool first.

- Don't keep leftovers too long in the refrigerator. I make "leftover soup."

- Put complementary leftovers in a pot with veggies and beef or chicken broth.

- Bleach, disinfect, or change kitchen cloths or sponges often, especially after raw meat, poultry, or fish has been prepared.

- Wipe the tops of all cans before opening them.

- Keep pets away from food, dishes, and work surfaces.

- Keep your hands and all equipment clean.

- Never use a knife with which you have cut raw meat or fish to cut anything else without first washing it thoroughly.

- Scrub chopping boards and worktop counters between uses.

- Keep separate boards for chopping raw meat and vegetables or cooked meat.

- Always store cooked food or any salad items separately from raw meats.

- Disinfect all work surfaces and the sink regularly, and especially all cloths used for washing up and/or wiping down surfaces, as these can transfer germs readily.

- Never wipe your hands on towels that are used for drying dishes.

9

Don't Throw In the Towel

One of the great selling features of our home at the beach was the abundance of space allocated for the laundry room. The area is roomy and has overhead skylights and a long folding countertop.

Doing laundry is less of a chore and can fit into even the busiest schedules when good equipment is close by. The area for the laundry can be anywhere. All you need is access to electricity, plumbing, drainage, and a vent to the outside of the home.

Good Space Saves Time

You will find that the chore of laundry goes much more quickly if you make the most of the storage and counter space you have available. Convert a closet into a laundry room with stackable storage units. Install racks for laundry supplies on the back of the closet door. If your washer and dryer are closed off by louvered bifold doors, install racks and deep shelves above the appliances for supplies. Vinyl-coated mesh shelving units, available at home building supply stores, are a practical storage solution.

Install a closet rod for clothes that should drip dry or that should hang immediately after they are removed from the dryer. Locate the rack as close to the washer as possible.

If space allows, build in a counter for folding and sorting your clothes; include open shelves for sorting bins. Store an ironing board and iron in the laundry room. If you have a choice, floor plans with separate laundry rooms are ideal for storage and organization. Often washing clothes becomes such an awesome, time-consuming task because we cannot keep up with the volume that needs to be cleaned. It seems like as soon as we get one batch processed, we have to start all over again. If we don't have some organization in this area of our lives, it will cause us a lot of frustration.

> She selects wool and flax and
> works with eager hands....She
> sets about her work vigorously; her
> arms are strong for her tasks.
>
> PROVERBS 31:13,17

Share the Load

Laundry is an ideal area of responsibility that can be delegated to other members of the family. I made it a point of teaching each of our children to do their own laundry by the time they were in the sixth grade. There's no reason you have to do all the laundry. Later in life, your children will call you blessed for teaching them how to care for their own things.

Teach children the basics of laundering.

- Recognize clothes that need special care.
- Sort clothes into three piles: white, darks, and colored.
- Set the proper controls on the washer and dryer.
- Determine how much detergent is needed.
- Use spot and stain removers properly.

SIMPLE IDEAS

- White vinegar will remove permanent creases when re-hemming pants or skirts. Simply dampen with vinegar and press with a warm iron.

- Plan your wash days and start washing early in the day.

- If your steam iron clogs, fill it with a mixture of ¼ cup vinegar and 1 cup water and let it stand overnight. Heat the iron the next day. Remove the mixture and rinse with clear water.

- Wash full loads rather than small ones. This saves energy—and your appliances.

- Hang a whisk broom on a hook beneath your ironing board. Use it to remove lint when pressing clothes.

- Use ironing time wisely—pray for the person whose clothes you are ironing.

- Remove clothes as soon as the dryer stops and then hang and fold. Clothes will be less wrinkled, and many times you won't have to iron items.

- Place sweaters in drawers or on shelves instead of hangers to prevent stretching.

- To make your blankets fluffier, add 2 cups of white vinegar to rinse water.

- To freshen laundry, add 1/3 cup baking soda to the wash or rinse cycle. Clothes will smell sweeter and cleaner.

- Don't use bleach and ammonia in the same wash. The combination can create hazardous fumes.

- Wear rubber gloves when hand washing with bleach.

- Add detergent or soap as the water fills, and then add the clothes.

- Do not put items in your dryer that are spotted with or have been in contact with paint, machine oil, gasoline, or any flammable fluids or solids. They are fire hazards, and their fumes can ignite. Line dry instead.

Storage

> In the long run, men [women]
> hit only what they aim at.
> Therefore, they had better
> aim at something high.
>
> — HENRY DAVID THOREAU

10

Reorganizing Space

Each of us has some interior decorating abilities. And at some point in time, many of us will want to reorganize our home—remove a wall, add a window, put in a door, remodel, add a new stairway, or add new kitchen cupboards. With today's spiraling real estate costs, remodeling and reorganizing is a practical alternative.

If a home doesn't function well, there are three choices:

- Learn to live with it.
- Move to a more suitable home.
- Alter it so that it gives the extra living space and the additional features needed.

The Changes That Make All the Difference

The average home is basically a box, within which internal partitions create rooms, doors allow movement, windows let in light and air, and systems (plumbing, electrical, heating/cooling) function. All of these can be altered to reorganize space.

In planning the reorganization of these features, there are two considerations which should constantly be in mind:

1. Are the changes feasible?
2. Are they legal?

Check with your local building department to see what, if any, permits are required for the work desired.

Alterations are usually made to a home's space with the intention of creating an entirely new living space or changing the present layout of the interior to improve various services and functions. Either way, reorganizing space can bring dramatic improvements to the way the house works. The following are a few of the changes that provide more efficient space and flow to a house's design.

1. Create a through-room. This requires removing an existing dividing wall and may require the repositioning of existing doorways and the relocation of windows. This will demand structural engineering to make sure proper beams (both steel and wood) are still present to carry the loads of the new floor plan.

2. Partition an existing room. Dividing an existing room into two smaller ones involves building a new wall, possibly adding a door or window to one of the rooms, and perhaps altering or extending existing plumbing, heating, and electrical services to serve the separate rooms.

3. Make a new door opening. Check to see if the area requires extra headers, depending upon the new door being in a non-load-bearing or a load-bearing wall. This alteration will probably require some replastering and touch-up paint (consider a new color, even).

4. Alter the kitchen layout. The amount of work depends on how extensive the arrangement will be. At the very least, there will be new base and wall cabinets and countertops. When repositioning sinks, stoves, refrigerators, dishwashers, there will have to be alterations to plumbing and electrical services.

SIMPLE IDEAS

- Look at your home in a new way. Imagine the possibilities and potential of your living space.

- Simplify and unclutter your life by saying no to good things and saving your yeses for the best things in life.

- Any system of organization must be right for you. There is no best way to be organized. Whatever methods you select must fit your lifestyle.

- In order to have order, you must figure out what your goals and purposes are in life.

- I have found that my motto "Do the worst first" helps me get started. Once the worst is done, everything else is so much easier.

- Share your goals with people who really care about you.

- Take advantage of visiting model homes or tours of homes. Write down features you'd like in your home.

11

Storage Solutions

When it comes time to organize your home, evaluate the big picture first, and then break the big into little, manageable steps. Evaluation of the big picture helps you to wisely determine how to shift items to create space, improve function of areas, and increase storage for effectiveness and efficiency.

If children pile their schoolbooks and homework assignments on the dining room table, it is time to create work space in their bedrooms. By doing this, you free up the dining room table and they have better space to do their schoolwork. If your closet is jammed full of clothes, you might want to consider installing double-hung rods. You also can store out-of-season clothes in an unused bedroom closet or build a wardrobe in the corner of the garage.

As you look at the big picture, you might consider building bookcases or hanging shelves to display your books and family picture groupings. When space is limited, use attractive bins and boxes to store and conceal personal papers, bills, and work or school projects.

Basic Storage Helpers

A few simple additions to your home will help increase your storage space. All of these can easily be found in home improvement stores, and they are easy to install.

- *Hooks and pegs*—In the early history of America before closets were built into our homes, the early settlers used pegs to hang their clothes. Hooks and pegs come in a variety of styles and materials and are just as practical today.

- *Moveable shelving*—Check with your local home furnishing store to see what's available. This type of shelving comes in a wide range of widths and tiers. It works well for bringing items stored in the rear of a shelf to the front. Older people find this idea very beneficial because they don't have to bend down far to see what's on a shelf.

- *In-wall display areas*—In between wall studs, carve out a shallow cavity to display items. This home improvement idea can be ideal for a kitchen or bath area where many small items, such as spices or toiletries, are stored. Space on each side of a fireplace is a great place to build such shelves.

Forgotten spaces in the home can be turned into valuable storage.

- *Under the stairs*—This is often overlooked space that can be used to house your excess overages. This space can be fitted with pull-out or standard shelving that can house all kinds of items.

- *Around windows and doors*—These areas are great for building attractive shelves to store books and collector items. Be sure your building material is thick enough and strong enough to handle the weight of what it will be holding. The top of a window seat can be built with hinges for out-of-the-way storage.

- *Built-in seating for the kitchen*—In small areas of the kitchen or dining area, you can pick up valuable space by including a built-in seating area in your design and remodel. Have the design include space underneath to store excess items.

One of the easiest ways to get more space is to have less stuff. Clear away the old and make room for new things or just the luxury and pleasure of open space.

- *Have a garage sale*—Even though you might say, "Who would want to buy my junk?" you would be surprised at what people will buy. Designate one area in the garage or basement for storage of these items. Before you place clothes in this area, make sure you wash and fold them neatly. Have your basic stationery items on hand so you can price and identify each article before you store it. When the garage sale weekend arrives, you'll have a big task already out of the way.

   Everyone's time is valuable. You might want to hire a professional to help you with your garage sale. Check in the yellow pages of your phone directory to see if there are any listings. If not, check with a few antique stores. They can probably help locate a professional.

- *Give items away*—Not only can you provide needed items to those who are less fortunate than you are, you can obtain a limited tax credit, and you can de-clutter your home. Check with your charity to see if they will pick up at your location, and whether they accept furniture. Keep a list of your donations, the condition of each item, and a receipt from your organization. You might even want to take a picture of the item(s) you donate (particularly if the item has value).

- *Take items to consignment stores*—These businesses are very popular. Locate a shop that resells clothing and home furnishings. Clothing must be clean and in good condition. Furniture and appliances must be in working order. The owner will charge you a certain percentage of sales for their service.

- *Sell on eBay*—You may not have the expertise to personally sell on eBay, but there are local businesses that are popping up around the country who will do everything for you. Be sure to investigate the particulars before you haul all your items to their place of business. They, again, will charge you a percentage for their services.

Remember that by using small bits of time faithfully, you can accomplish great things.

Where to Put the Towels

Our hallway closet used to be brimming with one thing—towels, towels, and more towels. It is easy to accumulate them over time. Some women keep frayed ones to use as cleaning rags or to use to dry off pets or dirty floors when kids track in mud. This is a functional idea, but it is also helpful to reduce the number of towels you have so that they do not take over your valuable space. Here are some other ways to store the towels that remain after you have tossed those that have seen better days.

- *Roll them*—Keep towels in a basket or rattan wine rack.
- *Rod them*—Increase hanging space by installing a long closet rod the length of the tub wall.
- *Rack them*—Use hotel-type racks that stow towels horizontally.
- *Hook them*—Install pegs instead of bars (which your family probably never uses anyway), and you'll have room for many extra towels. Put name tags above the pegs to help family and guests know which towel is whose.
- *Bar them*—Install a rod behind each bedroom door and have family members hang big towels in their bedrooms to dry. This eliminates clutter, reduces bathroom moisture, and humidifies the bedroom.
- *Toss them*—Do away with towels entirely. Give everyone in the family a terry robe that they can hang on a hook in their own room. You won't be washing a lot of bath towels—just the terry robes once a week.

SIMPLE IDEAS

- Things should be placed where they are most convenient. Store like items together: coffee tools and equipment, gardening supplies, laundry and sewing items, outdoor picnicking supplies, athletic equipment.

- Things you use often should be easy to see.

- Things needed at the same time should be in the same place (for example, store your stationery items next to your stamps, pens, and stapler).

- Everything should have its own place. Get away from forming stacks and piles. Remember: Don't put it down; put it away.

- Label containers. Take away the mystery of what is in all those boxes.

- Replace a single hanging bar with several bars at different heights. Jackets, blouses, trousers, and skirts can be hung in tiers.

- Build high shelves to store items that are used only occasionally or seasonally, leaving lower shelves and storage areas for more frequently used items.

- Build shelves or cubbyholes to accommodate shoes, sweaters, bulky clothing, and sports equipment.

- Fit children's closets with adjustable rods to "grow" with the child.

- Think creatively. If there isn't enough room for bed linens in a hall or bedroom closet, put them in an empty dining room sideboard. Or place Christmas items on the top shelf in the pantry.

12

Organizing Those Drawers and Closets

Make a habit to return everything to its proper place and remind others to do the same. If you do this daily, it takes less time than waiting until the situation is out of control. An even bigger bonus is that you won't spend time looking for out-of-place objects.

Now let's get down to serious business and get into our dresser drawers and closets. Let's weed out some of those things we don't need or use anymore. The idea "one comes in and one goes out" is an excellent reminder that when we buy something new, something else goes to the garage sale box or is given away to a favorite charity.

Drawer and closet cleaning is an excellent project for the whole family. Determine a weekend date that all family members will commit to. Write the date on the calendar and don't cancel unless it is a real emergency. Have Dad work in his areas and the older children work in their areas. Make sure they understand the basic principle of give away, put away, and throw away. I will discuss this in more detail later in this chapter.

There is a great deal of satisfaction and accomplishment when we have these areas under control.

Getting Started

When organizing, I highly recommend using "Put Away," "Give Away," and "Throw Away" bags. In our home, we walk into each area to be rearranged and take everything from the shelves, drawers, closets, and cabinets. As we pull stuff out of these areas, we keep in mind that if we haven't used or worn it for the past year (unless it's a garage item) it goes in one of these three bags. I suggest you use heavy-duty plastic black bags. Black bags are a must—this prevents others from looking at the sacks and saying, "Mom, you can't give that away."

Either you're going to put it away somewhere else, or you're going to give it away to somebody else, or you're going to throw it away.

Taking Inventory

Now let's start taking inventory of what you have. You can get real serious and use a sheet of paper that has headings such as:

- blouses
- shirts
- pants
- suits
- socks
- sweaters
- jackets
- shoes
- gowns
- underwear
- ties
- dresses

You might want to lay out clothes by category on the top of the bed or on a clean floor so that you get a bird's-eye view of what is overstocked and what is lacking.

Everything in Its Place

Hang your things up as you put them back into your closet. Each item should have a definite place. For example, all your extra hangers can go at the left end of your clothes pole. Then arrange all your blouses according to color, then your dresses, pants, etc. If you have a jacket that matches your pants, separate them. Hang the jacket with the jackets and the pants with the pants. This way you can mix or match your things and not always wear the same jacket and pants together.

Your shoes can go on a shoe rack. Separate them into dress, casual, and sport shoes. Break the habit of just throwing them into a corner. You might make sure your dress shoes are shined before you put them away.

I find that sweaters are best stored in clear plastic zipper bags. Belts and ties should go on hooks or on a rack designed for such storage.

Wire hangers are messy and crease clothing. Replace them with plastic, cloth-covered, or wooden hangers for dress pants, men's trousers, suits, sport jackets, or sport clothing. Slacks and trousers can be hung on clothespin-type clip hangers.

To save space in the closet, you might consider those hangers that can hold several pair of pants or trousers. Space savers are always good, particularly when most of us have limited wardrobes.

I find that dresser drawers need to be reorganized and weeded out of overstocked items. Toss worn out socks and underwear. Refold T-shirts. Put like items together; socks with socks, underwear with underwear. Set a two-hour time limit for this scheduled reorganization day. Any longer and you will lose the troops. Reward the family with a special meal for dinner.

SIMPLE IDEAS

- If your closets are small, add freestanding storage pieces, such as an armoire for hanging clothes.

- Double rods are great in wardrobes to hang shirts, pants, and suits.

- Attach pegs, hooks, or racks to the inside of the closet doors to make extra storage for hats, ties, and belts.

- The backs of closet doors also can hold racks or cloth pouches for shoes and small items.

- Get shoes, luggage, and other items off the floor. Use shoe racks, shelves, and hanging bags.

- Store little-used items, such as luggage, under the bed or in a utility area.

- Organize shelf space by stacking sweaters and storage boxes.

- Replace sliding closet doors with easier-to-access bifold doors. Paint the doors to match your room paint.

- Build shelving, drawers, or rod space into dormer areas.

- Place a comfortable chair near your closet to make slipping on shoes easier.

13

Helps for Kitchen Storage

The kitchen is a gathering place for family, friends, and guests to meet and enjoy each other's presence. The heart of a good home—the most rewarding part of a woman's domain and family responsibilities—is the kitchen.

Storage is the key to how well your kitchen functions. What kind of storage and how much you need depends on the size of your family, how much you cook, your lifestyle, and your cooking style. There are a few questions you should ask yourself before you get started:

- Where does your family eat most of its meals?
- Is it convenient to keep table linens, dinnerware, and flatware in this area?
- Do you like to do a special type of cooking?
- Do you do a lot of entertaining?
- Do you cook primarily from the freezer or the pantry?
- Do you need space for refrigerated and unrefrigerated fresh goods?
- Do you prefer clean, uncluttered countertops?

- Do you need cookbook storage?
- What appliances do you use?
- Do you like utensils, small appliances, glasses, cups, and other small items within easy reach?

Review the answers to the above questions, and you will grasp an idea of how you use your kitchen and what kind of storage space you may need. While a lot of the newer homes seem to have included a lot of storage, shelving, and pantry space that a twenty-first century homemaker may need, many of us live in older homes with limited space in the kitchen.

The key to acquiring more space in your kitchen is to get rid of excess clutter. Not only does this give you more room in which to work, it also makes for easier cleaning. If you don't have a place to store something in the kitchen, consider not purchasing it (or get rid of it if you don't use the item on a regular basis).

When limited space is a problem, I find that overflow boxes work well. I place items such as picnic utensils, Thanksgiving and Christmas pots, plates, and table settings into these boxes and store them in the garage, attic, basement, and spare room—even under the beds.

To maximize your space in this area of your home, you might consider:

- *Pantry area*—Carve out a pantry from a very small wall space. When space is narrow but deep, fit the space with pull-out shelving to put items at your fingertips. Install shallow shelves between wall studs to store cans one row deep.

  Store rice, beans, flour, cornmeal, cereal, and dry staples in sealed see-through containers—that way you'll always know their supply levels. Also, use containers for small packets of sauce mixes that can get lost in the pantry. Square containers are more space-efficient than round containers.

- *Cabinets and shelves*—Consider options other than standard base cabinets. Standard cabinets are cheaper to build and install, but custom-made cabinets with both deep and shallow drawers may better organize kitchen items. Plates and bowls can be stored in drawers if you use dividers. Existing cabinets can be remodeled with drawers and shelves that pull out. Check your options with your local cabinet maker.

- *Clever space savers*—Here are several ways you can save space in the kitchen:
    - Keep appliances you use each day on the counter.
    - Hang utensils from wall-mounted Peg-Board or hooks.
    - Put larger utensils in a Crock-Pot and store on the counter.
    - Mount a narrow shelf on the backsplash to keep salt and pepper, mugs, and frequently used items off the counter.
    - Hang a shelf over a window.
    - Purchase a corner cupboard for open storage.
    - Install plate racks around your kitchen walls where space permits.
    - Check local home centers, discount stores, and shops specializing in organizing for a wide selection of products.
    - Use drawer dividers for utensils.
    - Add lazy Susans to make corners accessible.
    - Purchase a multitiered plate rack to keep everyday plates handy.
    - Use wicker baskets to display frequently used flatware and napkins.
    - Use a chrome-plated steel basket with handles to keep fresh fruit neatly arranged, or store kitchen towels in a simple wire basket.

Must-Have Kitchen Equipment

Don't do without the basic tools that make homemaking and cooking easier. Spend several dollars and buy yourself can openers, quality pots and pans, and a few other things to keep the kitchen a pleasant place in which to work.

- *Mortar and pestle*—We use a mortar and pestle for garlic all the time to make a puree that can go very easily and smoothly into a mayonnaise. A mortar and pestle blends and presses the flavors together, which is very different from chopping.

- *Sharp knives*—All work in the kitchen is made easy with some sharp knives. You don't need a whole range, but it's important to use the right knife for the right purpose. How many should you have? I think you need a boning knife, a chef's knife—it could be smaller or larger, depending on what you feel comfortable with—and a couple little paring knives. And, of course, you need a serrated bread knife, which works for a lot of other things too.

    My knives are stainless steel. I never use knives that react to the ingredients (garlic and shallots, for instance, are especially sensitive to carbon steel). The fewer knives you have, the more care you can take sharpening and keeping them clean. The best way to sharpen knives is with a sharpening stone.

Make the kitchen the place to be. Make it fun and enjoyable. Learn to delegate some jobs to other members of the family. Plan to teach your children how to use appliances and kitchen utensils. This will allow them to be comfortable in the kitchen, and they will be better helpers at mealtime.

SIMPLE IDEAS

- Install plastic berry baskets in the pantry wall or on the inside of a cabinet door to hold small packages of sauce mixes, seasoning, and cold drink mixes.

- Hang mugs on cup hooks underneath your cabinet to save shelf space.

- Cut the lid off an egg carton and place the cups in a kitchen drawer. You can organize your nails, paper clips, thumbtacks, and other small items in them.

- To cover kitchen cabinet shelves, apply easy-to-install vinyl floor squares by just peeling off the backing. They are particularly good for lower shelves where pots and pans are usually stored.

- Place the plastic lids from coffee cans under bottles of cooking oil to keep cabinets clean. When the lids get dirty, just throw them away.

- A rubber-coated plate rack makes a great cookbook holder.

- Fit cabinet doors with racks to easily find cookware lids and canned goods. This is also a good space-stretcher for a small pantry. Install a rack for trash bags.

- Organize shelves with revolving racks for spices and other staple ingredients.

- Store rarely used items in large bowls or crocks arranged along cabinet tops.

- Add a baker's rack or cupboard to create a mini butler's pantry. Shop for a baker's rack with wide lower shelves for a convenient serving counter.

- No island? Buy a butcher-block cart on wheels from a specialty kitchen shop. It is easy to move around the kitchen, and it gives you added storage space.

14

A Wrapper's Delight

Some people think they need expensive store-bought gift wrap in order to have an attractive package, but they don't. With a little creativity, we can learn to dress last-minute presents with what's around the house.

If you're out of store-bought wrapping paper, try construction paper, newsprint, or nonadhesive drawer liners. The sheet should be wide enough to overlap on the box's top by two inches and just long enough to cover its ends. Costume jewelry, buttons, and wallpaper scraps can give gifts a festive flair. Or you can doodle with paint or rubber stamps.

You can always use plain white wrapping paper and add a little flair with sponge printing, rubber stamping, and finger painting.

If bows are in short supply, use colored twine or hair ribbons. Raffia adds a very casual and charming accent to your gift. Young men and boys love the appearance of a gift that's wrapped with brown wrapping paper and a raffia tie. Feel free to tie on generous lengths of brightly colored yarn for a warm and fuzzy touch.

Wrapping Dos and Don'ts

1. Do experiment with colors and textures. Don't be afraid to mix polka dots, stripes, and florals together.
2. Do give a hint as to the contents of the gift with a little peek-a-boo gift tied to the ribbon. An individually wrapped tea bag on a package containing a set of tea cups, a set of chopsticks on a wrapped Asian-print scarf, or a bar of soap on a set of guest towels.
3. Do use double-stick tape. Nothing ruins the look of a package as much as a long piece of scotch tape laid across the joining seam.
4. Do use sharp scissors to cut ribbon. You don't want ribbon edges to be frayed or roughly cut.
5. Don't feel you have to conceal every gift in paper. If you give a gift that has beautiful packaging like a box of note cards, a nice ribbon with a tag is all you need to make an impression.

Gift Tags

Making your own gift tags adds personality to any gift. A simple way to create them is to use small scraps of gift wrap and fold them to card size. Almost any object on which you can write or paint can be used as a tag: wooden spoons, ornaments, paper dolls, cookie dough cutters, key chains, shells, and bookmarks. Paint pens, which can be bought at craft stores, write on almost anything and the color and print won't come off.

Tying extra items to the package with ribbons or bows is a lot of fun. If possible, capitalize on a hobby or vocation of the person who will receive the gift. For the golfer, use some golf tees tied onto the bow; an artist, a new brush; the mechanic, a new tool; the gardener, a new pair of gloves or seeds; the craft lady or knitter, knitting needles or embroidery thread tied onto the bow.

Here are some more package add-on ideas: Flowers—silk, real, or paper—and leaves and pods, seeds, pinecones, nuts, a nosegay made out of doilies and flowers, evergreens, holly, mistletoe, bells, jingle bells, tree ornaments, sewing notions, spools of thread, batteries (especially on those gifts that will require them), office supplies, school supplies, and potpourri in lace bags tied with a bow.

Children will love this gift idea. Roll up a dollar bill (or more) and insert it into a balloon. Mail it along with a card and instructions to blow up the balloon and then pop it. Out comes the bill!

Organize Gift Wrapping Supplies

Let's take the stress out of wrapping gifts by organizing all the supplies we need to do the job creatively and quickly. The ideal tool to help busy women is the "perfect gift wrap organizer."

This organizer contains all the wrapping supplies you need including:

- scissors
- tape—double-stick for packages
- mailing tape—filament reinforced
- wrapping papers—rolled gift wrap is best because there are no seams and less waste
- clear cellophane
- kraft paper—great for rubber stamping and sticker art

It's a Wrap

There are plenty of resources in your home that can be used as wrapping and package adornments. Take a look at just a few of these. Use your imagination.

- shelf paper
- wallpaper
- newspaper—funnies, sports page, stock market section, travel section
- fabric
- tissue paper—white, colors, plain, polka dot, graph, or patterned

- gift boxes—enameled, fold-up, acrylic, or Lucite
- gift bags and totes—lunch bags, enamel bags, cellophane bags, window bags, small bottle and jar bags
- tags or enclosure cards
- ribbon—satin, plaid, taffeta, curling ribbon, curly satin, fabric, rickrack, shoelaces, measuring tape, lace, jute
- stickers
- mailing labels
- glue gun, glue sticks
- chenille stems—use on your make-ahead bows and store for future use
- rubber stamps, stamp pad, or brush markers
- homemade ribbons—make your own with pieces of leftover fabric. Almost any type of fabric can be cut to the desired width and length. Striped materials are great to cut into even widths. Then press fabric between sheets of wax paper with a hot iron. This will keep the strips from unraveling and provides enough stiffness for the ribbon to hold its shape when making it into a bow.

Revitalize Old Wrapping Paper and Bows

- Make used wrapping paper new again by lightly spraying the wrong side with spray starch and press with a warm iron.
- Run wrinkled ribbon through a hot curling iron to take out old creases.

Cellophane Is the Answer

- "How am I going to wrap that?" gifts are perfect to cover with cellophane.
- When wrapping a basket, bucket, pail, or small wagon toy filled

with goodies, tie cellophane with a bow and a bit of holly or pine, or use stickers.

- Cellophane is the perfect covering for food, whether the present is a Christmas plate full of cookies, a basket of bread, a basket of muffins in a checked napkin, or muffins in a muffin tin.
- Use cellophane to cover a nice plant.
- Wrap a fresh bouquet of flowers with clear or colored cellophane. Tie with a beautiful bow and a special note inside.

Gift Bags

- Decorative or decorated gift bags are a wonderful idea for a quick, easy wrap! And they are reusable, either for you or the recipient.
- Line gift bags with contrasting tissue or wrap your gift in tissue. Add a bow to the handle with a gift tag. Add shredded tissue on top for a festive look. (Use any color combination depending on the time of the year and cut tissue into ¼ inch strips, toss like a green salad, and you've made "tissue toss.") Decorate bag with stickers, banners, or cutouts from old Christmas cards.
- Large silver, black, or green plastic garbage bags may be just the thing to hide a large gift. Add a banner, large bow, and stickers. It will look like Santa's pack.

Gift Boxes and Containers

- The beauty of gift boxes is that the decorated ones need only a ribbon!
- Always ask for a courtesy box, tissue, and ribbon whenever you buy anything at a department store or where the gift wrap is free. Save them in your gift wrap center for the times you need them. Usually they fold flat and are easy to store.

- Use tins, ceramic containers, Lucite or acrylic boxes, flowerpots, buckets, pails, and baskets as your present's container.

Gift Certificates

- Purchase blank certificates from craft or stationery stores.
- Make your own with calligraphy, sticker art, or rubber stamp art and then laminate them. Have certificates redeemable for babysitting, dinners at your home, frozen yogurt, plays, movies, days of shopping and lunch, etc.
- Keep some gift certificates on hand to favorite bookstores and coffee shops. These make great last-minute gifts or can be used as a package add-on.

SIMPLE IDEAS

- Pay attention to your wrapping paper seams. Corners should be carefully creased and the folding style you use on one end should be repeated on the other end.
- Think about the gift recipient and personalize the gift according to their taste and personality.
- Add inexpensive letter charms representing the recipient's initials to bows or packages.
- Keep scraps of paper and fabrics. If you have a strip of expensive, patterned paper or fabric, use it to create a band around a gift wrapped in a solid color for a modern artsy look.
- Be sure your ribbons don't have creases or wrinkles. Iron the ribbon (use very low heat) before tying it on your gift.
- Check with your local party store to obtain valuable hints and beneficial supplies to help you become a delightful wrapper.

SECTION FOUR

Finance

If you collect enough pennies
you'll eventually be rich.

— JOHN WOODEN

15

Value Your Worth

In our various seminars on marriage and relationships, we point out that there are emotional, physical, and psychological differences between men and women. There are also some financial differences.

- Women generally underrate the value of their labor.
- Until recently, women have had difficulty in making certain financial transactions because of policies, attitudes, or restrictions.
- Approximately 50 percent of marriages end up in divorce, with women usually getting the children and the financial burden for raising them.
- Most Americans living below the poverty line are women.

Historically, women's pay scales have been less than men's. This is changing as women pursue roles which have usually been held by men, such as engineers, construction workers, attorneys, doctors, truck drivers, and so on.

In order to break away from past limitations, there are several things we can do.

1. Improve Your Financial Position Now

- *Increase your base salary.* You may have to ask your boss for a raise, take a second job, or develop a hobby into a paying endeavor.

- *Create your own line of credit.* Maintain a good credit record with your telephone company, utility company, and a gasoline credit card. Make sure you have a good reference with your bank by having both a savings and a checking account. Build a good credit history by establishing a department store charge account, adding an oil company credit card if you don't have one in your name, and applying for a small loan to be backed up by your signature or collateral. These accounts are only to help you establish credit in your name. Don't get into debt beyond your ability to pay. Great discipline must be used in developing this strategy.

- *Protect your principal.* Be cautious with your money and don't speculate with your investments. You want assets, not losses.

2. Improve Your Financial Self-Worth in the Workplace

Surveys show that girls rate the importance of boys' labor higher than their own. Interestingly, boys rate girls' work equal to their own. It appears that our culture has trained women to think less of their labor. However, don't underrate yourself. Begin with a fair appraisal of your worth to your company. If you feel you are carrying your part in making the company profitable, you should ask for a raise, ask for a job with more responsibility and with more pay, or begin to look for a better job.

There are certain steps you can take to get a pay increase:

- *Take an inventory of your good points.* Write them down on paper. Why are you valuable to your company? How have you expanded your job?

- *Decide how much you are worth.* Do a salary survey on your own to see how much others are making in your same job.

- *Ask for the raise.* If you are stalled, ask again. Here are a couple of reminders of what not to do:

- Don't threaten to quit. If you want to leave, just give your notice (make sure you have a new job first, if possible).

- Don't change your mind once you have given notice.

- Be professional and don't complain with the other employees.

- Don't be angry, but feel good about the decision you make.

3. Take Steps to Get a Better-Paying Job

There are certain positions within a company that more directly contribute to profitability than others. Where does your job fit into contributing to that profitability? You may want to change job classifications in order to be more important to your company or to a new company. You might want to:

- *Go into sales.* Direct sales of a company's product will pay you more than being a sales clerk. Executive sales pays excellently, and it's a field where more and more women excel. As long as you can sell you will be rewarded.

- *Pursue more education if needed.* Many communities have continuing education in evening classes in all areas of vocation. If you don't have a bachelor of arts degree, you might want to consider enrolling in a nearby college or university.

- *Learn a skill that pays well.* There are many such careers available in computer information, service industry, dental and medical assistance, etc.

- *Start your own business.* Your can start from scratch or enter into the vast field of multilevel marketing companies. This type of business will reward you according to your production. Be sure to do your research before joining any organization.

SIMPLE IDEAS

- Scripture is filled with wisdom, ideas, and guidelines for understanding and managing money and resources.

- The rich rule over the poor, and the borrower is servant to the lender. —Proverbs 22:7

- Make all you can, save all you can, give all you can. —John Wesley

- If anyone does not provide for his own, and especially for those of his household, he has denied the faith and is worse than an unbeliever. —1 Timothy 5:8 NKJV

- How much better is wisdom than gold, and understanding than silver! —Proverbs 16:16 TLB

- He who gathers money little by little makes it grow. —Proverbs 13:11

- Much is required from those to whom much is given, for their responsibility is greater. —Luke 12:48 TLB

- And if you are untrustworthy about worldly wealth, who will trust you with the true riches of heaven? —Luke 16:11 TLB

- Plans fail for lack of counsel, but with many advisers they succeed. —Proverbs 15:22

16

Cornerstones for Money Management

∞

A very good friend of ours, Jim, is a bricklayer par excellence. All of the most discriminating homeowners in town smile with pride when Jim can do their masonry work. He is so good that recently the California Brick Association selected him as the outstanding builder for using brick as a building material. Jim has done brickwork for us in each of our homes over the last 20 years. He is the best in his profession.

The first thing Jim does when he gets to the job location is make sure he knows where the cornerstone is going to be. Everything will be built from this central calculation. All heights of retaining walls will originate from here. Several years ago we had a new garage built, and the contractor did the same measuring and calculating to determine the four cornerstones and to make sure they would be level.

Are you someone who just can't pass up a good deal: that special high-tech equipment, another camera gadget, one more power tool, another set of golf clubs, or an all-weather coat you can't do without?

We've all had that extra impulse that makes us go deeper into debt, slowly sinking our money ship. Even though these all seem like small expenditures, they are rarely necessary and they always add up financially. But if we measure our actions in relation to the cornerstones for money management, we can avoid miscalculations.

Four Cornerstones for Money Management

Cornerstone 1: Recognize that God owns everything. He owns our homes, our cars, our marriages, our children, our jobs, our businesses, and our talents. We may possess them, but we don't own them. Possession is not ownership. In Haggai 2:8, God states, "The silver is mine and the gold is mine." Psalm 24:1 properly states, "The earth is the LORD's, and all it contains, the world, and those who dwell in it" (NASB). Everything belongs to God. We are merely stewards of His property. God holds us personally responsible to faithfully manage for Him whatever money or possessions He allows us to have.

Often we are tempted to grasp our possessions selfishly, as if they actually belonged to us and not to God. I'll never forget the beautiful blue 1972 Mercedes Benz we cherished for about ten years. Bob waxed it often to keep it shining brightly. He kept it in the garage when I wasn't driving it, and he dusted it every day.

Once when we were away for a few days, our son, Brad, and a few buddies came home from college to go skiing. Brad saw our Mercedes in the garage and decided to take it to the mountains to impress his friends and any young ladies they might meet. He strapped the ski rack to the roof, loaded the skis and poles onto the rack, and headed for the slopes.

All went well until they started home. The ski rack vibrated loose and slid off, leaving a dent and a large scratch on the roof of our car. When we returned home, Brad broke the news. When I saw the damage I was angry at Brad for taking our car without asking and devastated that he had allowed our prized car to be damaged. It didn't take long for me to regain my composure. God was using the incident to test our perspective on our car. "Well, God, Your car has a scratch and a dent," we said. We drove God's scratched and dented car for another year and a half. Each time we looked at the damage, it reminded us who really owned the car.

As caretakers of God's money and property, we must obediently grow and nurture the spiritual fruit of self-control.

Take a few minutes and jot down your possessions that God owns.

1. *my marriage* 4. *Endeavor / wk truck*
2. *house* 5. *jobs*
3. *children* 6. *talents*

If you have never given them to God before, you might want to do that now. Turn everything over to Him.

Cornerstone 2: The goal of financial responsibility is financial freedom. In order to be financially free, you must meet these qualifications:

- Your income exceeds your expenses.
- You are able to pay your debts as they fall due.
- You have no unpaid bills.
- Above all, you are content at your present income level.

If you are not satisfied with what you have, you will never be satisfied with what you want.

List three things you intend to do to become more financially free.

1. *Pay off cash call*
2. *sell montero*
3. *change wk sch. so we don't need daycare for Emily*

Cornerstone 3: Establish a spiritual purpose for your life. If your spiritual purpose is to serve God, all of your resources become ministering currency toward that end. The more money we give to God's work, the more our hearts will be fixed on Him. The opposite is also true: Don't give money to God's work, and your heart will not be fixed on Him. An example of this principle comes from Patrick Morley in his book *The Man in the Mirror.* He shares about when his family first experienced an increase in their monetary resources. Their greater disposable income logically caused them to think a newer, bigger, nicer home was the next step.

> The social pressure to buy the bigger house preoccupied my mind. The image of having money, and making sure everyone else knows it, pulls like a tug-of-war against the Christian life view.
>
> One day I noticed I was the only family member pressing for the move. That got me thinking. Finally I yielded my ambition to move to the bigger house and allowed God to work. We decided to redecorate instead.
>
> Over the years we began to give shape and form to the belief that God wanted us to put a cap on our standard of living. And however He blessed us over and above that standard of living, He wanted us to help fulfill His purposes.
>
> This decision evolved. We didn't actually sit down and write it out on a piece of paper. Rather, over time, by our lifestyles and actions, we inbred it into values. Then one day we said it out loud, and that settled the issue.
>
> So now we live a predetermined standard of living. And everything God entrusts to us above what we need to live and save for retirement, we give to His work. I would have guessed that living in a bigger house would have made me feel more significant. Yet the sense of usefulness and the impact that we are having leaves us with a deep confidence that we are truly significant, not for our own self-gratification, but in a way that will last forever.[1]

Write down several areas of your life where you could change priorities and direct the monies to God's work.

1. *eating out/entertainment*
2.
3.
4.

Cornerstone 4: Give money to the Lord on a regular basis. Once I heard a comic on TV say, "I've been rich and I've been poor, and I like being rich better." For the Christian, the only reason to be rich is to have resources to carry on God's program. Does God need our wealth? No. Can God's purposes be carried out without our money? Yes! God doesn't need our possessions, but we do need to give.

God doesn't care how much we give as deeply as He cares *why* we give. When we lovingly and obediently fulfill our role as givers—no matter what the amount—God will use what we give to minister to others, and we will receive a blessing in return. The Scriptures clearly show us many directions for giving:

- to God through our tithes, gifts, and offerings (Proverbs 3:9-10; 1 Corinthians 16:2)
- to the poor (Proverbs 19:17)
- to other believers in need (Romans 12:13; Galatians 6:9-10)
- to those who minister to us (Galatians 6:6; 1 Timothy 5:17-18)
- to widows (1 Timothy 5:3-16)
- to family members (1 Timothy 5:8)

Godly Principles of Giving

On the subject of giving to God, we have already determined that everything we have is His anyway. The question of how much we should give back to Him in tithes, gifts, and offerings is debatable among Christians. Some insist on a "tithe" (10 percent), and others claim that grace allows each individual to give as he chooses. Without entering the debate, my point is simply that Christians are clearly instructed to return to the Owner of everything a portion of what He has given to us.

Second Corinthians 9:6-15 contains three excellent principles on the topic of giving. Read the passage for yourself and note the following principles:

Principle 1: We reap what we sow. If we sow sparingly, we will reap sparingly. Plants cannot grow if no seeds have been planted. Cups cannot overflow unless liquid is continually poured into them. If you want an abundance, you must give an abundance. If you give little, you will reap little.

Principle 2: We are to be cheerful givers. We are not to give because we feel pressured to give, but we are to give freely and joyfully as in all other areas of ministry. We have attended a couple of churches that have helped worshipers grasp this truth. In one California church, no offering plates are passed. The church leaders believe that if God is working in your life, you will make the effort to place your gift in the mail slot in the wall. Another church we attended called the offering box in the foyer the "blessing box." Leaders in this church taught the principles of giving and then trusted parishioners to respond to God's Word instead of an offering plate. Whenever a special financial need arose, the elders brought it to the congregation and the need was met.

> Stewardship is the acceptance
> from God of personal responsibility
> for all of life and life's affairs.
>
> ROSWELL C. LONG

Principle 3: We will be blessed because of our obedience. The world will know we are obedient to God by our faithfulness in giving. You may ask, "How can I give before I receive? Don't I need to have something before I can give it?" That may be the way we think, but that's not the way God thinks. Luke 6:38 states, "Give, and it will be given to you." Only after we give are we ready to receive what God has for us.

Many people wonder, "What is the right way to give money to the Lord?" I was raised with the concept of the ten percent tithe, and that has been our guideline for returning a portion of our monies to God's work, both in the local church and to parachurch organizations. This money needs to be set aside as it is earned and then given in a systematic way each Sunday. (Even when away from the church on a Sunday, we need to continue to give on a regular basis.)

There are many Christian businessmen and women who give tithes of their companies' earnings to Christian organizations. We have a builder in our city who builds a new church each year as his way of returning profits back to the Lord. These tithes are to be used in the work of the local church, but God may direct you to help other worthwhile groups that aren't church affiliated.

Your giving should be done in private to guard you against becoming proud or trying to control an agenda on where it should go. Remember, we are giving to God and not to man, and so we should not look for a blessing from specific churches or people to whom we give.

To reach the end of the month without asking the famous question, "Where did all my money go?" you need to:

- Recognize that God owns everything.
- Strive for financial freedom.
- Establish a spiritual purpose for your life.
- Give to the Lord's work regularly.

"You may say to yourself, 'My power and the strength of my hands have produced this wealth for me.' But remember the LORD your God, for it is he who gives you the ability to produce wealth" (Deuteronomy 8:17-18).

Common Financial Mistakes

In addition to the principles for money management, let's look at some common financial mistakes that can cost us a lot of money.

Mistake 1: Attempting to get rich too fast. There is no quick way to get rich. If it's too good to be true, it's probably not true. Stay away from quick ways to make a dollar. So many folks have been taken in by smooth-talking salespeople. Build up sales resistance by saying no often.

Mistake 2: Believing the credit-card delusion. Credit on credit cards does not mean you have a higher standard of living—it could be the eventual ruin of your finances. With rare exceptions, don't charge any more than you can pay off when the bill comes due.

Mistake 3: Not taking advantage of your benefit plans at work. Most companies offer employee 401(k) or 403(b) saving plans that permit you to avoid paying current taxes while saving money for retirement. Talk to your personnel office at work to see if your company has such a plan. If not, consider opening your own IRA plan.

Mistake 4: Overpaying your house payment (mortgage). If you didn't refinance your home mortgage recently when interest rates were at an all-time low, you are probably overpaying your monthly mortgage. You may be able to reduce your house payment significantly by refinancing. Shop around to see what interest rates are available. Start out with your present lender and go from there.

Mistake 5: Paying too much for insurance (auto, home, life, and health). Review with each of your carriers to see if you can reduce your premiums. In some cases you may be buying more coverage than you need. This also provides an opportunity to reevaluate where you need more coverage.

Mistake 6: Investing for your children's college education the wrong way. Because tax laws and education savings incentives vary from year to year, it's important for you to consult your tax advisor or bank representative to discuss your options and establish the best plan for you.

Mistake 7: Falling for a "hot tip." Avoid these with a passion. Don't invest your hard-earned money in anything you don't understand. Never be swayed by a phone solicitor. Only deal with reputable parties—and make sure you understand the offering and the risk. Request a copy of the prospectus. Read it thoroughly, and ask questions before you give any money.

Money Management Practices to Follow

1. *Maintain excellent credit.* Protect this status as if it were gold. If your credit report contains incorrect information, take care of that immediately. If you do not, such incorrect data could delay or prevent you from getting a loan or delay the refinancing of your home mortgage. There are several online services that will give you your up-to-date credit report free of charge. Due to reporting and processing variances, your credit report may not be identical at each of the credit bureaus.

You are entitled to a free credit report every 12 months from leading credit reporting agencies. Call toll-free at (877) 322-8228 or check out www.annualcreditreport.com. I suggest you stagger your requests by several months to provide the maximum information on your current status.

2. *Keep your money invested in areas that provide good returns.* If most of your money is in no- or low-interest checking or money market accounts, think about shifting that money into five-year CDs or purchasing U.S. Treasury EE bonds. For a small risk, consider short-term bond funds or short-term U.S. Treasury notes. Call a good brokerage firm in your area for more information. Many banks also offer this service.

3. *Keep good financial records.* Your system doesn't have to be fancy, but your records need to be saved in a fashion where you can be sure to deduct the expenses on your tax return. Keep track of home improvements so you will have proof of these expenses when you get ready to sell your home. Listing home improvement costs may decrease tax on your capital gain. All it takes is a simple log recording the date of each improvement, what it was, how much it cost, and a running total in the last column—very easy, and it takes just a few minutes. Be sure to keep receipts for these improvements.

4. *Record your credit cards.* We all assume we will never lose or have our credit cards stolen. When they are lost, you scurry to hunt for the credit card issuer so you can call them and notify them of such an event. In a file folder marked "Credit Card Info" record all the pertinent information regarding each credit card. List the name of the company, card number, company address and phone number, and expiration date for each card.

5. *If married, make sure your mate is part of the money management process.* I have friends whose husbands died, and they knew very little about the family's finances. Make sure you are involved in these decisions and know what's happening.

6. *Be willing to take a few risks.* This is different than the "too-good-to-be-true" story. A well-balanced portfolio will have a diversified approach to stocks, bonds, CDs, real estate, and money market accounts. Consider

keeping some of your savings in investments with growth potential. You can choose stocks or mutual funds for some of your personal savings. Again, check with your bank representative or stockbroker.

7. *Prepare a trust, a will, and a living will.* Contact a local attorney who specializes in estate planning and set up a date and time for your meeting. This is so very important in order to leave your estate to those you want to benefit from your lifetime of work. Shop around to compare fees. The range of charges can be surprising.

SIMPLE IDEAS

- Warning signals if you are having money problems:

  o Your current monthly bank statement balance is considerably lower than your previous statement balance.

  o Your current credit card totals are significantly higher than on the previous statement.

  o The amount you budgeted for household cash disappears faster than usual.

  o Your expenses are greater than your income.

- If cashing a check, wait to endorse it until you are at the bank; otherwise, it can easily be cashed if it falls into the wrong hands. When depositing, add "for deposit only" on the back of the check. This helps to ensure that if lost the check cannot be cashed, only deposited.

- ATM machines are convenient, but they should be used with care. If the machine is in a secluded area, avoid it. Be aware of other patrons; if anyone looks suspicious, leave immediately.

- If you make a mistake while writing a check, correct it neatly and initial the change. Write in permanent ink.

- Start cutting out some unnecessary luxuries or bad habits from your daily routine. For example, buying a large mocha five times a week instead of a large black coffee can cost around $500 extra each year.

- Consider consolidating debt through a home equity line of credit or refinancing your mortgage.

17

Staying Out of Debt

While riding with our tax attorney a few years ago, we pulled up to a stoplight and Bob commented to Al, "Look at all of these expensive cars." Al looked over with a grin and stated, "Bob, most of these drivers are so deeply in debt!" He should know because each year during tax season, he works 18 hours a day meeting with clients to prepare their returns.

Americans are consumers. We love to spend, spend, spend. For many people, their sense of worth depends upon their ability to purchase and have stuff. If we do not have enough money from wages, we create a false lifestyle by purchasing with credit cards. Consequently, many of our possessions end up owning us when we cannot afford them in the first place. They become a burden or a demand, and they can drain our resources if we do not pay attention.

> If you have not been trustworthy
> in handling worldly wealth, who
> will trust you with true riches?
>
> LUKE 16:11

Financial pressures cause a lot of the divorces in our country. Money-related dilemmas destroy family unity. But how do we get out of debt when we find ourselves in trouble? You can face debt head-on as a couple or independently. But either way, the piper has to be paid.

Of course, the soundest advice is to never get caught in a situation of bad or overextended credit in the first place. However, if you are in this hole, how do you get out? Here are seven steps to easing the burden and eventually the existence of debt.

1. *Take inventory of where you are.* The first step of recovery is to realize you have a problem. After you recognize that a monster is in your home, you must take a realistic inventory of how much debt is owed. In order to do this, list out the following figures:

- mortgage payment
- credit cards (all of them)
- balances of other loans (list each separately)

Don't include food, clothing, school costs, utilities, taxes, etc.

Once all of these expenses are written down, establish a plan for repayment. Ask God to give you the strength to be faithful in all of your responsibilities and obligations. Then ask Him, "What do You want to teach me in this situation?" God's plan doesn't include us being slaves to our debtors; He wants us to be free from all the negative strains that debt plays on our whole being—even our spiritual status.

2. *Stop your old, bad habits.* The best way to not be in debt is to avoid going into debt. Using the credit card to buy nonessential items must stop immediately. Old habits have to be extinguished. It may have taken years to get in trouble, but you have to begin a solution now. No time to waste. I find it unrealistic to burn, cut, freeze, or melt all your credit cards, because there are certain transactions that must be made with credit cards. So be selective in which card you will keep. Most merchants will accept one of the big three: Visa, Discover, and MasterCard.

If you decide to cancel a card, be sure to notify the credit card company. If not, they will continue to bill you for the yearly renewal (if your card carries an annual fee). However, you will still be responsible for any debt you have remaining.

Contact someone to hold you responsible for your use of a credit card. In fact, you might make a pact with this individual that they will review the use of your card before you use it. They will discuss whether you really need the items in the first place.

Ask God to help you be accountable on not going further into debt.

3. *Make a plan for repayment.* Before you can do this, you must figure out what your monthly living expenses are. List out the following and total the figures:

- monthly mortgage $
- insurance needs $
- food costs $
- clothing costs $
- utilities $
- taxes $

You can come up with these figures by going back over your previous month's statements and arriving at a total figure for your monthly expenses. Take this number and subtract it from your monthly income. This is the amount of money you have left over for paying off your debt.

4. *Make the most of your money.* While many of us may feel broke by the end of the month, we often have places where we could cut some fat from our spending routines. Take time to examine your spending and determine where you overlook extra fees or hidden costs and where you overindulge on things that might not be priorities.

- *Cut living expenses.* You have to go bare-bone on expenses. Things such as entertainment, clothing, food, trips, cable television, coffee, and eating out for lunch must all be reviewed and cut. The savings in this area can be added to debt repayment.

- *Review your tax withholding.* Meet with your employer to see if you can decrease some of the money taken out of your paycheck each month. If you always get a tax refund, it means you are overpaying your taxes, and that money could be used to pay off debt.

- *Sell things.* A garage sale will give you some money to go toward debt repayment. You may even have to consider larger items such as an extra car, a TV set you don't use, an extra refrigerator in the garage. You must make a commitment to do what you can to get out of debt. Make a pact that you will make a significant lifestyle change if necessary.

- *Double up payments.* Most of your minimum payment goes to interest and not to principal. Double up on your payments so that the second amount can be applied to the principal. By doubling up on payments and cutting extra lifestyle spending, you can quickly reduce the balance due on the loan.

- *Pay off smallest loan first.* By paying off the smallest debt first, you can then take that monthly payment and add it to the next smallest credit card debt. Paying off even one credit card or other source of debt will make you feel great.

- *Keep your commitment to the Lord.* Proverbs 3:9 tells us to "Honor the LORD with your wealth." Giving must be a top priority for us. When you remember this commitment to God, your stewardship will be blessed. When we give our firstfruits, we are recognizing that God owns everything.

5. *Be accountable to someone.* You might want to go to some person you respect and ask them if they would be willing to review your plans. If you are involved in a local church, you might go to a church leader and ask for accountability assistance. One of our favorite mottoes is: "It's not what you expect but what you inspect." It's good to have someone come alongside and inspect your plan of action. Several minds are better than one. Be honest and up front with those you ask to help you. They must not be surprised by information you didn't reveal. Be willing to be transparent about your real situation.

6. *Dedicate your finances to God.* Many blessings in Scripture are promised to people who dedicate their finances to God (that means assets as well as liabilities).

- His master said to him, "Well done, good and faithful servant; you have been faithful over a little, I will set you over much; enter into the joy of your master" (Matthew 25:21 RSV).

- Honor the LORD with your possessions, and with the firstfruits of all your increase; so shall your barns be filled with plenty, and your vats will overflow with new wine (Proverbs 3:9-10 NKJV).

- My God shall supply all your needs according to His riches in glory in Christ Jesus (Philippians 4:19 NASB).

- Instruct those who are rich in this present world not to be conceited or to fix their hope on the uncertainty of riches, but on God, who richly supplies us with all things to enjoy (1 Timothy 6:17 NASB).

- Owe nothing to anyone except to love one another, for he who loves his neighbor has fulfilled the law (Romans 13:8 NASB).

7. *Celebrate!* Rewards are a strong motivator to do a job well. As you pay off each of your cards, you might think about what would encourage you to keep your commitment to yourself. Maybe a lunch, maybe a new dress, maybe a new piece of jewelry would inspire you. Remember, you don't want to go further in debt. These rewards don't have to cost a lot; they are something to look forward to. The biggest reward will be when you are no longer in debt.

SIMPLE IDEAS

- Even after you've paid off a loan, continue paying out the same amount to your own savings account each month.

- If your salary is paid or credited by direct deposit, some banks will waive certain fees.

- To conserve money, pay cash for things you'll soon use up, such as food items and cleaning supplies. Use credit only for things you'll continue to use after you've finished paying for them or for emergencies such as medical bills.

• It pays to use "cents off" coupons when buying food. Little by little, the savings add up over time.

• Pack a sack lunch if you work away from home. You can save a lot of money over a period of several months.

18

Keeping Track of the Numbers

Managing our money involves more than just staying out of or paying off debt. I hope you will reach a time when you won't have debt to keep track of, but you will always have basic functions of money management to take care of. Doing taxes and balancing a checkbook probably rate about the same on most women's list of least favorite things to do—in the top five!

Doing my taxes each year is something I mentally gear up for. I recommend hiring a good CPA because they know the tax code and can always save you more than if you did the filing of the forms yourself. However, I know many people who prefer to do taxes themselves. You might want to consider the following when you fill out your own forms.

- *Keep it simple.* Use forms 1040EZ and 1040A if you make less than $100,000 and don't itemize deductions.
- *New car sales tax.* Be sure to remember your large sales tax deductions—a new car, a boat, large-scale home renovations. Be sure to save your sales receipts for verification.
- *Child care credit.* Take the allowable deductions for child care costs per child.

- *Did you start a new business?* Check with your IRS office, but if you started a new business after October 22, 2004, you may be able to deduct $5,000 for start-up costs and $5,000 for administration costs during the first year and amortize the remaining costs over 15 years.

- *Sale of stocks.* If you sold any stocks this last year, be sure to check with your CPA and let him or her know of any losses or gains so that proper calculations can be made.

- *Track your mileage.* If you have any unreimbursed business travel, make sure you deduct the allowable rate per mile. Be sure you have a log with notations regarding the actual data, such as date, destination, purpose for trip, starting and ending miles, total miles driven.

- *Nonprofit contributions.* As often as possible, pay your contributions by check or credit card. Avoid cash because you have no way to verify amounts. If you give clothing, furniture, equipment to a nonprofit organization ask for a receipt and note the approximate value of gift.

- *Equipment and furniture.* As a home business, you can amortize the costs of any new equipment or furniture which you may have purchased. Be sure you have your receipts on record.

- *Entertainment.* If you are a small business owner, you may have occasion to take out a client for lunch to discuss business. Save your receipt, and on the back record whom you met and what was discussed.

- *Energy efficiency.* If you have purchased a hybrid car, check to see if you are entitled to deduct $2,000 for it. Some states also allow a deduction for the purchase of energy-efficient appliances.

Be on the lookout for any tax saving ideas that might appear in your local newspaper as tax time gets near. Every deduction you are entitled to is to your advantage.

The Balancing Act

It is amazing how many people do not balance their checkbooks. With the convenience of ATM machines and online services, consumers rely on the bank to provide them with the bottom line numbers. But when we depend on others to tell us how much money we have or to tell us exactly where our money is at all times, we have surrendered the management control of our resources. And keep in mind that banks, computers, and the people entering data do make mistakes sometimes.

Balancing your checkbook can be one of the important exercises in money management. In our home, Bob takes care of all the banking for our family expenses and all the finances relating to our ministry. He balances both checkbooks.

An absolute rule in our home is to reconcile the bank statements within 48 hours of receiving them. Keeping these up-to-date is very important. Reconcile each monthly statement by using the form found on the back of your statement. If the check is for an item that is tax deductible at the end of the year, make a copy of this check and file it in your "taxes" manila folder. If you don't have access to a copy machine, you can put a red "T" in the upper right-hand corner of the check for simple referencing. At tax time you have quick access to a copy of these and can easily make calculations for your federal and state tax returns. I also photocopy all checks which I need for future verification of major purchases, stock purchases, and contract agreements.

Before you start, be sure you have entered all transactions in your checkbook, including interest earned, electronic activity, and bank charges as shown on your statement. The steps in reconciling your bank statements are:

1. Be certain all your deposits were recorded correctly. Compare your deposit receipts with the deposit entries on your state-ment.

2. Be certain the correct check amounts are deducted from your bank balance. Compare each check returned in your statement envelope or noted in your check register to the amount deducted by the bank on your statement. Anything that doesn't agree is a bank error.

3. Identify checks that have not been deducted from your account. Just check off with a red pen in your check register all checks

returned with your statement. Any check register entries not marked are outstanding checks you have written that were not received by the bank by the time your statement was prepared. These outstanding checks must be deducted from the balance shown on your statement to determine the actual balance in your account at the present time.

4. Identify and deduct bank charges. Your bank will charge you for anything it can, including NSF (nonsufficient funds) checks, ATM usage, or a monthly account charge. Deduct the total of these charges (once you are certain they are correct) in your check register to adjust your actual balance. By the same token, add any amounts credited to you for interest-bearing accounts and/or deposits you have made after the statement date.

5. Contact your bank immediately if you find any errors in your account.

Sample Reconciliation Form

1. Enter deposits not shown on this statement (including electronic).

Date of Deposit   Amount
Total A:

2. Enter all checks, all withdrawals (including electronic), and any bank charges not shown on this statement.

Outstanding Item/Check No.   Amount
Total B:

Ending balance on your statement: $

Total A: +

                                     = _____

Total B: - _____

Current Balance   = _____

(This should equal your checkbook balance.)

If you reconcile each statement, you will know what your balance is at all times. You won't need to call the bank or keep checking online. This kind of knowledge keeps you in charge and in control of your money.

Canceled Checks

There are several ways to maintain a proper record of the canceled checks. They are:

- Store them in a manila file folder labeled "Bank Account."
- Store them in a separate check file box intended just for canceled checks.
- File checks in order by check number, along with deposit slips, deposit receipts, and your check register.
- Don't leave canceled checks and statements lying loose in a drawer.
- Don't assume that your statement is accurate just because the process is computerized. Errors can be made.

SIMPLE IDEAS

- Money management is really more about your attitude toward the use of money than a systematic plan to which you become a servant.
- As a rule of thumb, the maximum amount of credit and installment debt payable monthly should never be more than 40 percent of your monthly gross salary (before deductions).
- As an alternative to banks, don't forget your credit union. They usually charge less for most loans and pay more interest on savings accounts.
- To avoid too many family expenditures occurring simultaneously, stagger the medical and dental checkups of family members.
- When a repair estimate is more than 15 percent of an appliance's replacement cost, seriously consider buying a new appliance.
- It makes sense to refinance your home mortgage if the old rate is two percent more than the new loan interest rate.

19

Be Smart at the Supermarket

∽

Unmasking the art of shopping for food is one of the great discoveries for a homemaker. Marketing techniques become more sophisticated each year. The large chain stores have to be so competitive, which can, in turn, provide some benefits to shoppers in the form of discounts, bulk sales, membership benefits, and more.

Thankfully, my Bob has always loved to shop for our food. He likes looking for good deals. Comparison shopping is a challenge to see the differences in cost between one manufacturer and another. The Sunday morning paper gets scoured to find coupons that can be used for the next shopping trip. The two stores that we shop at give double coupons. There are times Bob leaves the market and his cost savings are 30 to 50 percent by using coupons. I have a good friend whose wife doesn't think much of coupons, so he shops and uses all kinds of cost-saving opportunities. The money he saves he puts in a special account. When hunting season comes, he often buys new equipment and pays for his hunting trips out of this fund created from monies he has saved by being smart at the supermarket.

We use the provided shopping list when we go to the market. If I discipline myself to stick with the list, it has two benefits: saves me money and speeds up my shopping. The longer you stay in the store, the more money you will spend.

Shopping Checklist

FROZEN FOOD/JUICE

	QTY	Cost	Coup
Ice Cream			
Vegetables			
Prepared Dinners			
Juice			

CONDIMENTS

	QTY	Cost	Coup
Syrup			
Molasses			
Jelly/Jam			
Peanut Butter			
Honey			
Shortening			
Oil			
Catsup			
Mustard			
Vinegar			
Mayonnaise			
Pickles			
Relish			
Salad Dressing			
Croutons			

CANNED GOODS

	QTY	Cost	Coup
Soups			
Canned Meat			
Tuna			
Canned Meals			

CANNED VEGETABLES

	QTY	Cost	Coup
Tomato Sauce/Paste			
Vegetables			

STAPLES

	QTY	Cost	Coup
Flour			
Sugar			
Cereal			
Nuts			
Jell-O			

SPICES

	QTY	Cost	Coup
Bacon Bits			
Coconut			
Chocolate			
Baking Soda			
Baking Powder			
Salt/Pepper			

PASTA

	QTY	Cost	Coup
Spaghetti			
Pasta			
Rice			
Instant Potatoes			
Mixes			

DRINKS

	QTY	Cost	Coup
Coffee			
Tea			
Juice			
Sparkling Colas			

PASTRY

	QTY	Cost	Coup
Crackers			
Cookies			
Chips			
Breads			

Buns

	QTY	Cost	Coup
Buns			

PAPER GOODS

	QTY	Cost	Coup
Paper Towels			
Tissue (Facial)			
Toilet Paper			
Napkins			
Plastic Wrap			
Waxed Paper			
Foil			
Trash Bags			
Zip Bags:			
Small			
Large			

HOUSEHOLD

	QTY	Cost	Coup
Dishwasher Soap			
Dish Soap			
Clothes Soap			
Bleach			
White			
Colors			
Fabric Softener			
Furniture Polish			
Lightbulbs			
Vacuum Bags			
Pet Food			

MEAT

	QTY	Cost	Coup
Beef			
Chicken			

Certain tips can help you become a better and wiser shopper. Regardless of where you do it, smart shopping is savvy shopping. Here's how to spend smart time in your supermarket.

1. *Watch the ads.* Most major newspapers will have a shoppers' section on Thursdays and Saturdays. Look for and cut out any discounted ads. Often you can pick up a circular as you enter the market. Often these will list sales items that aren't listed anyplace else.

2. *Money and minute savers.* Everything used to have to be made from scratch, but not necessarily anymore. Brownie mixes can be cheaper to make than baking from scratch. Faster too!

3. *Try nonbrand items.* Be a risk taker and try an off-brand label. Many of the store brands are the same, but they have different packaging. Different packaging leads to less advertising costs, which leads to cheaper prices.

4. *Select fresh, high-quality foods.* Consider these smart shopping tips from the University of Wisconsin Extension Service:

   • Always use your senses when shopping (eyes, nose, and fingertips—when appropriate) to determine the freshness of raw meats and produce.

   • Avoid items that are in torn, dented, or damaged containers.

   • Make sure refrigerated and frozen foods are below the cold line in their cases.

   • Buy cold and frozen foods last, right before you check out.

   • Put meat, poultry, or fish in plastic bags so they don't drip on your other groceries.

5. *Be a comparative shopper.* Compare prices first before you buy and then choose which one you think is the better value. If on sale, don't frown on brown eggs. They have the same nutritional value as white eggs. Ready-to-serve soup is usually triple the price of condensed soup or broth made from a dried mix. When you

see "two for $5.00" be sure it is an actual deal. Ask the checker if they will sell you one for $2.50 if that is all you need.

6. *Clip coupons.* Coupons are a great way to save on your shopping bill. Most stores will honor and give you double value for the face value. Don't be embarrassed because you carry around an envelope with coupons. After all, the markets would not honor them if it wasn't profitable for them.

7. *Get in and out.* One of the values of making a shopping list is you get what you need and get out of the store. The longer you spend at the market, the higher your bill will be. Use the shopping list I have provided or create one of your own.

8. *Watch for meat sales.* Meat seems to be the most expensive food purchased. Taking advantage of sales on meats can help keep your food costs under control. Some shoppers don't select or plan their dinner menus until they see what's on sale at the market.

9. *Shop during the best part of the day.* Plan to shop during the best shopping hours. The best time is early in the morning or later in the evenings. Early Saturday morning seems to be the best-of-the-best. The store will be well-stocked, fully staffed, and not as crowded.

10. *Buy your postage stamps at the market.* Save yourself a trip to the post office. Most large markets sell stamps at the same price they are at the post office. This will save you a stop while on your errand trip.

SIMPLE IDEAS

- Peruse the top and bottom shelves—the best buys are often placed above or below eye-level range.

- Prevent a bag from spilling its contents by securing it with a seat belt.

- A laundry basket in the trunk of your car is a good way to store your bags on the way home. Things will stay upright and gathered together, and you'll make fewer trips from the car to the kitchen when you get home.

- Bigger is not always better. Take advantage of bulk buys only if the size is practical.

- Check the close out or discontinued shelves if your market has them. Often bakery goods will be displayed.

- For "fill-in" trips, don't buy more than you can check out in the express lane.

- Pack all freezer and refrigerator items together to keep them cold for the ride home. You'll also save time unloading the goods.

Family Time

If I cannot give my children
a perfect mother I can at least give
them more of the one they've got—
and make that one more loving.
I will be available. I will take time
to listen, time to play, time to be home
when they arrive from school,
time to counsel and encourage.

— RUTH BELL GRAHAM

20

Safety Tips for Working Parents and Their Children

A popular movie a few years ago was *Home Alone*. It depicted a child who was left behind at home while the parents journeyed off on a vacation. They didn't realize their son was not with them until they were far away. The rest of the movie dealt with the extreme troubles a child can get into when parents are not there.

It can be frightening, confusing, and even dangerous for children to be home by themselves. There are millions of children who come home after school and, in many cases, wait several hours alone. These kids are often referred to as latchkey children.

What can parents do to prepare children for this situation? Below are some suggestions that will help you and your child. Having a plan in action will save you time and ensure safety when the situation arises.

Rule One: Establish clear expectations and home routines. Make sure you explain rules for these times when children are alone. Make homework a top priority by requiring that it be completed before the TV or computer can be turned on.

Discuss whether they can leave the home, have friends visit, or talk on the telephone. Spend plenty of time discussing the ground rules. Reevaluate the guidelines from time to time.

Rule Two: Plan family conferences. Always keep lines of communication open. It's very important that we remain transparent. These valuable times can be used to review the last week's events and to go over the calendar for the next week. Make sure they understand your schedule in case your routine will be different from normal. Communication helps to reduce any last-minute panic. Make sure the children are aware of dates and times they need to know about, such as ballet lessons, sports practice, or doctors appointments. A master calendar is a great tool to use during family meetings and to have posted at eye level for the children.

Rule Three: Be realistic in your guidelines. Children will be children, and they will not always be perfect. They can be given more responsibility when they exhibit they can be trusted with more responsibilities. A rule that the child cannot watch television or talk on the phone is impractical. After all, there needs to be freedom in the home while they are alone. Nutrition should be addressed and planned for. Fruit, vegetables, yogurt, and snacks need to be provided. Anticipate these needs.

Rule Four: Welcome your child home. Even though you might not be there when the child comes home, you can create a warm environment that says "Welcome" when they come through the front door. You can write a sweet note and leave it on the kitchen table or on the child's pillow in their bedroom. Leave a message on the answering machine to greet the child home. A surprise snack or special treat is always a nice greeting. Leave out a bag of microwave popcorn that can be placed in the microwave for a quick two-minute goodie. Allow a few minutes after they are expected to be home and give them a welcome home phone call.

Even a child is known by his actions, by whether his conduct is pure and right.

PROVERBS 20:11

Rule Five: Build connection between you and your children. A parent must think through very carefully how they can reassure their child. Tell kids that they are able to contact you immediately, even if you are in a meeting. Have the child visit where you work. This way they can visualize what your place of business looks like, and they get a feel for how long it takes you to get to and from work.

Rule Six: Go over phone etiquette and rules. Explain to the child that there are times when Mommy and Daddy may sound very businesslike when they call. Many times others are able to listen, and the conversation must be more formal. Train your child to answer the phone properly and to never say to an unacquainted caller that the parents aren't home. They can reply courteously, "My mom or dad can't come to the phone right now. May I have your name and number?" If a call seems scary, have them hang up immediately.

Every child should know how and when to call 9-1-1, the police, and the fire department.

Rule Seven: Contact a neighbor. In most neighborhoods there are a few neighbors who would be willing to help you and your child in case of an emergency. Ask permission to call upon them on an emergency basis only. Invite the couple or individual over to your home so your child can meet them and become acquainted. This way the child will feel more comfortable if a time should arise when they need help. Be sure your child has their name, address, and phone number handy along with the other emergency numbers.

Rule Eight: Teach your children to be careful around strangers. In today's society this is a very important skill to teach your children. Discuss with them that in case of an emergency they should turn to an adult (female preferred), a uniformed adult, a mother with children, a shop owner, etc. A stranger who approaches a child for any reason is always to be regarded with suspicion. Reject any offer that a stranger might make of your child, asking them to help solve his problem. Teach your child to never get into a stranger's car.

Rule Nine: Teach home safety. It's important your children understand how to treat an emergency if one should occur in the home. Tell them what to do in case of fire. Practice an escape route from each room in the home. Conduct monthly fire drills. If you live in an apartment, instruct the children to use the stairways for escape and not the elevators. The children should know that in the case of a fire, they should leave the home immediately. Their well-being is more important than the contents of the home.

Children have an abnormal attraction to matches. Discuss with them the danger and consequences of lighting matches inside the home.

Rule Ten: Make sure the children can believe you. If you promise your children you will be home at a certain time—make sure you are. If for any reason you will be late, call home and let them know of the delay. A few minutes may seem like a small deal to you, but for a child who is home waiting for a parent to come home, it's a very big deal. Keep your promises. You will also discover that if you abide by this rule early on, the children are more likely to follow the same courtesy when they are older. You will appreciate this when you are waiting for your teenager to return from a late night at work, a church activity, a school sporting event, or a date.

SIMPLE IDEAS

- Try creating a time-out by removing your child to a designated chair or area for a brief period (one minute for every year of age is the rule), solely for you and them to regroup.

- Take children outdoors and talk about playing safe. Define boundaries and show them how far they may go.

- Hang a bathroom mirror at the child's eye level if you want to start encouraging good hygiene and grooming habits at a young age.

- Have your young child dust and sweep along with you at first. The youngster will feel grown-up, and you'll get more work done.

- Clearly define the time of day when a child's job is to be completed— either before school, right after school, or by dinner.

- Never pay children for doing something for themselves. It robs them of self-esteem and is a form of bribery.

- The more we do for our children, the less they can do for themselves. The dependent child of today is destined to become the dependent spouse and parent of tomorrow.

- Take family walks as opportunities to talk about ideas, observations, and feelings.

- Encourage your children to begin saving a portion of their allowance by the time they are nine years old. You can encourage the habit by matching whatever your children save.

21

Single and Living Without Stress

In America today we see an increasing number of people who are single. They fall into one of three categories:

- Those who have never been married
- Those who are divorced
- Those whose spouse has died

The single person who has never been married is most often a young man or woman who is just getting started in the financial world. People are getting married later in life today; it is not uncommon to meet 35-year-olds still single by choice. This category of single usually doesn't have an income problem, but they do with outgo. If this is you, here are a few survival tips:

- *Establish income goals.* You have probably learned to live within your present income level. As a single you can do this with less adjustment than a married couple. Unfortunately, you may very well be adapting yourself to a low income by having inadequate savings, cutting back where you need not, and having insufficient

135

money for vacations. Revise your income goals to be more challenging than what they presently are.

- *Have a disciplined budget.* Know what you need to spend and
  then be sure to allocate your income accordingly.

- *Don't buy too much life insurance.* For single people I recommend
  buying a good term insurance policy that covers burial costs and
  any other expenses that might be incurred following death.

- *Have an adequate health insurance program.* If you work for a
  company with a group health insurance policy, this will usually
  be adequate. If you are self-employed, you will need to seek out
  a good agent who will advise you of adequate coverage.

- *Save and invest.* See our chapters dealing with this topic. There
  are excellent no-load or low-load growth-type mutual funds
  which you can invest in through a monthly investment plan.
  Don't invest in risky investments. Only go with a sound, financial
  adviser who comes highly recommended by personal referrals.

- *Control your expenses.* Be very careful on your outgo of money.
  Many singles can get into a very damaging habit of living beyond
  their means through splurging on luxury items.

- *Have tax-deferred retirement savings.* Because most single unmar-
  ried people are young, they think retirement is too far ahead to
  worry about. The time is now. Don't wait.

Life After Divorce

Being divorced is the most difficult of the three single categories.
In most cases both parties suffer financially, particularly if children are
involved. Women are often the single head of a household on an inadequate income. You will need to build or rebuild your career goals. Here
are a few things you can do to help the situation:

- Arrange a satisfactory alimony trust as part of the divorce settle-
  ment. Not everyone will have enough assets to fund this.

- You will not be able to maintain the same lifestyle as when you were married. Divorce always hurts financially. Both parties usually have to cut back.

- Be faithful to your responsibilities. Irresponsibility in these areas will be the beginning of many legal and financial woes.
- Make sure there is adequate insurance to protect against disaster.
- Have a savings account to cover emergencies.
- Have a living trust or will made.

Life as a Widow

Insurance charts indicate that most women will live eight years longer than their husbands. You will need to carry on when he is gone, so don't wait until it's too late. Begin today to learn basic survival knowledge around the house:

- where the electrical box is located
- where to turn off the gas and water
- where the list of repairmen is
- the location of savings and investments
- who handles the insurance policies
- a review of monthly payments
- basic repair skills to avoid having expensive repairmen come

There are scores of details that must be handled before the surviving spouse can carry on a normal daily routine. You might want to start a log to answer all these questions.

The largest percentage of Americans living below the poverty level is widows. Review your insurance and retirement benefits so you will have a basic understanding of the resources that will carry you through your remaining years.

Living Alone

Here are some tips that will help you live alone with peace of mind:

- Learn to live economically. Protect your savings and retirement funds. If you work, continue to save if possible.

- Use all the resources you are eligible for. If you qualify for tax breaks or other benefits, don't hesitate to take advantage of them.

- Maintain your health insurance. As you get older, this is one of your most important benefits.

- Have adequate life insurance coverage to pay for future illness and burial expenses.

- If you have spare bedrooms, you might want to look around for someone to live with you. This income will help offset your expenses and the situation will provide you with companionship.

- Have a current living trust or will made.

SIMPLE IDEAS

- Come...without money and without price. Why do you spend your money for that which is not bread? —Isaiah 55:1-2 RSV

- Resolve not to be poor: whatever you have, spend less. —Samuel Johnson

- The real measure of our wealth is how much we'd be worth if we lost all our money. —John Henry Jowett

- The moral problem of our age is concerned with the love of money, with the habitual appeal to the money motive in nine-tenths of the activities of life. —John Maynard Keynes

- The man [woman] who loves money is the man who has never grown up. —Robert Lynd

- Trust in your money and down you go! Trust in God and flourish as a tree. —Proverbs 11:28 TLB

- No man is really consecrated until his money is dedicated. —Roy L. Smith

- Nothing that is God's is obtainable by money. —Tertullian

22

Babysitting Survival Guide

Sixteen-year-old Christine arrives at the Whitney home, eager to take care of Bradley Joe and Weston. The parents, Bill and Jenny, chat for a few minutes with Christine. The couple is so glad to get out of the home and to be on their weekly date—just the two of them, no children and no dogs.

About 45 minutes later, two-year-old Weston is still crying and screaming "Mommy." Christine remembers that the parents were going to be at three different places during the evening, but she can't remember what time they would be where. She's not even sure if she should call.

Meanwhile, Bill and Jenny keep remembering things they wished they would have told Christine before leaving home. Their intimate conversation is interrupted by an ongoing debate about whether to call home.

There are certain steps to take to ensure a smoother and more enjoyable evening for sitter and parents alike. I call these survival hints. Over the years, from raising my own children to assisting our children raise our grandchildren, I have come up with a few guidelines that can be of help.

For Mom and Dad

- Leave a pad and pen by the phone to be used for phone messages and notes of the evening events.

- Have a first-time sitter arrive a little bit early so you and your children can get acquainted with each other. This gives the sitter the chance to become familiar with your home before you leave.

- Explain your home rules about snacking, visitors, television programs, music, and anything else important.

- Tell the sitter what time each child is to go to bed and whether a certain child has any special needs, such as medicine, a toy, a special animal, a blanket, or story time.

- Show the sitter, if necessary, procedures for feeding, warming the bottle, and diaper changing.

- If your child is to be given medication, have instructions as to time and dosage written down next to the bottle with a measuring spoon or dropper nearby.

- Let your sitter know at the time of hiring whether they will be expected to prepare and serve any meals or do dishes.

- Have a flashlight or candles handy in case of a power outage.

- If the sitter won't be able to easily reach you, plan to call home periodically.

- If you aren't able to arrive home when you said you would, call and let the sitter know you will be late and when you expect to arrive home.

- Always be prepared to pay the sitter the previously agreed upon fee when you return home unless you have worked out another agreement beforehand. Some parents pay extra for time after midnight.

- If you must cancel a sitter at the last minute, it is courteous to pay the sitter for part of the time they agreed to sit.

- If you want your sitter to do any housework, make special arrangements at the time you hire them. Most parents pay extra for this added service.

For the Babysitter

- Be sure you understand what is expected of you. Write it down. Don't count on your memory.
- Make sure you know what other adults can be reached if you have any questions.
- It is best if children are present when parents give you instructions so you all understand the rules.
- Don't open doors for strangers.
- Keep all outside doors locked at all times.
- Any deliveries can be left outside or delivered when the parents are home.
- Don't tell telephone callers that parents are not at home.
- Take a message when you answer the phone.
- Keep your personal calls very brief.
- Always clean up your own messes. Any extra effort will be appreciated by the parents.
- Don't snoop into their personal belongings.
- Try to stay alert and awake unless it is a long, late evening.
- Let the parents know of any illness, accidents, or items broken.
- If you have to cancel the appointment, be sure to contact the parents immediately.
- You might consider taking a basic Red Cross first aid class. You never know when you might need the information.

You might have this type of chart printed up for you and your sitter. The information will be a big help to you.

Notes for the Babysitter

We can be reached at: _____

We will be home about _____ o'clock.

A little about us

Our name: _____

Our address: _____

Our phone number: _____

Children's names: _____

Ages: _____

Emergency numbers

Doctor: _____

Dentist: _____

Police: _____

Fire/Rescue: _____

Poison Control: _____

Neighbor: _____

Special Instructions

Location of thermostat: _____

Instructions about pets: _____

Locations of children's food and clothing: _____

Children's habits: _____

Children behaved: _____ Above Average _____ Average

Comments:

SIMPLE IDEAS

- Never pay children for doing something for themselves.

- The happiest, best-adjusted individuals in their present and older lives are those who believe they have a strong measure of control over their lives.

- Assign a designated place where each child can study and a regular time to do his homework. Make sure there is plenty of light, ventilation, and quietness.

- If your family is uncooperative, consider whether your standards are too high. You may need to readjust your level of expectations.

- Take family outings so you have an opportunity to talk about current issues and any problems in the children's lives.

- Put on family plays. Ham it up in original skits with hand-me-down clothes.

- Make work fun. Children love to wear rubber gloves, chef's hats, and aprons, and use feather dusters, spray bottles, sponges, and child-sized mops and brooms.

23

Connect with Your Children

Parenting seems to become more difficult with each generation. Bob and I realize that raising healthy children today is more complicated and demanding than when we raised our two children. Every ten years, life becomes more complex, and this complexity makes it difficult to maintain balance while raising children. There are so many more demands on the family structure than ever before.

Connected by Faith

There is one fact that never changes—the importance of a faith foundation. Adopting a godly faith that encourages belief in God, developing a habit in regular attendance at a house of worship, and being part of a family that shares similar spiritual goals will create a foundation that encourages, nurtures, and unites a family.

We know that much of our success in raising Jenny and Brad and in supporting the raising of our five grandchildren is due to our participation in church and our connection to our faith.

> Prayer is something that is more
> caught than taught. Praying parents
> usually raise praying children.
>
> J. CARL LANEY

Connected by Communication

While there are no guarantees in parenting, I've experienced that the most spiritually grounded children have parents who truly enjoy listening to them. The following are some ideas that as a parent seemed to foster a close relationship with our children and now our five grandchildren:

- *All listening doesn't need fixing.* You don't have to have a solution for everything you hear. Often the children just want you to listen—no fixing required.

- *Look eye to eye.* When the children are young, you might have to get down on your knees, and as they get older you can stand. Eye contact is very important in order to be a good listener.

- *Stay in touch.* You might think that your child doesn't want to talk, but let them know you are always interested in their lives and you are always available.

- *You learn a lot through casual conversations.* Those short five-minute casual conversations are so valuable. Don't think that for a talk to have meaning it must go on for 30 to 60 minutes. Many times they don't have large blocks of time. Take what you can get.

- *Make conversation part of your family tradition.* That's why having an evening meal together is so valuable. These are times when each member of the family can share feelings and ideas. Children will talk when they have traditions of family time and sharing time in their lives.

- *Be positive in your language.* I've found that a minimum of criticizing is best if you want frequent conversations. Talk time should be a positive experience for both parties. Negative sessions aren't fun for anyone.

- *Maintain strict confidence.* You must be trusted by your children if you want them to come back again. What is said here stays here.

- *Stop what you're doing.* TVs go off, papers are put down, music level is turned down. Your conversation is the number one priority for the moment.

- *No assumptions allowed.* Hear out the whole situation before you come to any conclusion. It's easy to assume before you hear all the facts. Be sure to answer. Sometimes you might even have to say, "I'll get back with you."

- *Make sure you have warm body language.* Body language often says more than the verbal words uttered. Be cautious of how your nonverbal language comes across. Try to keep positive as you talk back and forth.

- *Answer without minimizing the situation.* To you the item discussed might be a small deal, but to them it's a biggy. Show signs that you are really identifying with their concern or situation.

- *You have ideas too.* Conversation with children isn't a one-way street. You have opinions and should feel free to express them. You might try asking these questions when you think there might be a proper break in the conversation.

    o *Is there anything else?*

    o *Would you like to know what I think?*

Sometimes you won't be able to talk everything out. It's okay to ask, "When can we get back together to discuss this topic?" Be sure to put the date and time on your calendar.

As I observe healthy families, I find that one thing they all have in common is good communication skills. Some families are higher energy than other families. This type of family requires more talkathons than the more kick-back families. Whatever your family style is, talk, talk, talk.

Everyone should be quick to listen, slow
to speak and slow to become angry,
for man's anger does not bring about
the righteous life that God desires.

JAMES 1:19

SIMPLE IDEAS

- Spend at least one hour per week one-on-one with each of your children.

- Send an occasional note to your children. Mail it if you can (children love to get mail).

- Tell each of your children every day that you love them.

- Love outwardly your children's father. They love to know that Mom and Dad love each other—offer affectionate words, hold hands, use good manners, take walks together.

- When the children want to talk, give them your 100 percent attention. Put down the paper, mute the TV (better yet, turn it off). Give positive body language.

- Remember children learn by action more than by words.

- Look eye to eye when talking to your children.

- Maintain a moderately pitched voice—keep from loud, boisterous tones.

- Tuck your children into bed and pray with them. Depending on the age of your children, read them a short story or book.

24

Assure Your Children that You Love Them

All parents have probably had one of their children ask, "Do you really love me?" If you haven't taken the time to think about a response, you may not be prepared to give reasons that satisfy the child. The easy way out is to say, "Yes, I love you." Children are always testing us to see if we really love them. They might:

- Make embarrassing sounds at the supermarket
- Wear strange clothes
- Color their hair with bright colors
- Hang out with the wrong crowd
- Run away from home
- Challenge your way of life

Each of these are signs of children crying out, "Do you really love me?" It seems strange that they would do negative things when they really want positive responses.

We who are organized swear by the idea that list makers are more organized than non-list makers. Making a to-do list, a shopping list, and an error list seem to be motivators for us to stop procrastinating and get off the couch. Here is a list that gives you essential ingredients for loving, successful parenting:

1. *Spend quality time with each of your children.* It seems as though we are always talking about quality vs. quantity. Most parents will agree that we need to spend time together. But are we doing things with our children which they enjoy (such as recreation)? Are we doing things that will build their character (such as work)? Are we leading them in activities that will build their spiritual lives (such as family devotions)?

My experience is that it is very important not only to spend quality time with our children as a group, but also to spend time with them individually. One-on-one contact helps and encourages better child-parent relationships.

Take a child out to breakfast, lunch, or dinner, just the two of you. This gives you both a time to let down your hair and share on a personal level because no one else in the family is around to interfere with the dialogue. I've also found that behavior and relationships improve when we meet like this. After such an occasion, you might want to schedule another outing. Be sure to put it on both of your calendars.

Having daily time together is also very important. Reading a story and praying together before bedtime are great relaxing times for the children. My 22-year-old granddaughter still asks me to tuck her in when she comes to visit and spend the night.

Let your children know that they are special to you and the family. A parting hug and a kiss lets them depart with a good feeling about parents and home.

2. *Show love for your husband.* Children feel more secure when they see that their parents love each other. Remember, each day we choose to love our mates. It's not what they do, but what we choose. When speaking to the children about Dad, make sure you are making him a hero. Brag about him, tell the children what the positives are about him. Ruth

Graham says, "Tell your husband the positive and tell God the negative." Be a cheerleader for your husband.

3. *Listen to your child.* God made us with one mouth and two ears. I guess He wanted us to listen twice as much as we talk. One of the most difficult communication skills is to be a good listener. For some reason we all think that what we have to say is more important than what the other person has to say. Children stop talking to their parents when they feel that Mom and Dad aren't listening to them. If your ears are bent in their direction, I can almost guarantee they will talk to you. They just want to know you are listening.

When a conversation is taking place, stop daydreaming about what needs to be done around the home or at the office. Immediately go eye to eye and focus your undivided attention upon what they are talking about.

Start early in their years to be a good listener, and you won't experience the typical generation gap that is shared by many families. The children will talk if you will listen. Bedtime is a great time to share quiet moments together. Go to their rooms, sit on the bed, read a story, say a prayer, and just wait for that special question they have been thinking about all day. If you give your conversations breathing room, children almost always get around to expressing themselves.

4. *Pray for and with your child.* Many great biographies are written by individuals who say, "I am who I am today because of having parents who prayed for me!" Be sure to include your children in your daily prayers. Don't stop when they leave home. When the apron string is cut, the prayer string continues. Praying children usually come from praying parents. Let the children catch you reading your Bible and praying. When your children know that Mom is praying for them, they will be reassured of your love and commitment. Deuteronomy 6:7 states, "You shall teach them [the principles of Scripture] diligently to your children, and shall talk of them when you sit in your house, and when you walk by the way, and when you lie down, and when you rise" (RSV). As parents we are to use every opportunity to share our faith with our family. Children love

to hear how God has answered prayers in your life. Let your faith story give them hope.

5. *Lead your children.* Stop being a friend to your children and become a parent. Our culture today wants everyone to be a friend. Adults don't need to take responsibility when they are friends, but they do if they are going to be a parent. Parents have to establish boundaries and set discipline when those guidelines are broken. Parents have to make unpopular decisions often, but they must believe that what and how they are teaching is for the good of their children.

As children mature and show that they are dependable, they can be granted more freedom. As a parent don't be afraid to set the boundaries within the family. Children feel secure when they know the boundaries, and when they realize you will stick to those boundaries.

Parents need to develop rules that will guide their children until they are sufficiently mature to make their own decisions. Parents are to lead and guide.

6. *Hug your child.* We are all brought up with different ways to express love one to another. Maybe your family members weren't huggers. Maybe this is hard for you to do, but let me encourage you to risk rejection. There's something about a warm bear hug that is so reassuring to a child. Yes, there will be times as children get older that they don't like being hugged in public, but that doesn't mean they don't like hugs in private. A hug is like a pat on the back that says "I love you."

7. *Read to your child.* We live in a world where high-tech gadgets have taken over. Everywhere you look children are wearing ear buds and headphones and blocking out the world. Begin to read to your children when they are babies. They love to cuddle up on the couch and get lost in your voice as you unlock the words on the pages of their favorite books.

As parents we should offer our children a wide variety in reading materials—Bible stories, fairy tales, history, missionary biographies, nature and wildlife stories. Reading unlocks the imagination and creativity of your children. They are able to ride off into sunsets they never knew existed.

As we read to our children on a consistent basis, they will begin to develop a love for books and a zeal for information. They will find that books give them a peace from all the world's stresses. This is a joy that will enrich their lives.

SIMPLE IDEAS

Home is about making the most out of your life and your family's life every day.

- Create a home and life you and your family enjoy.

- A well-organized, clean, and safe home creates a peaceful, comfortable environment for you and your family.

- There are no magic solutions, but with some thought and practice you can make a home that nurtures you and your family.

- Make your family and home your top priority.

- A home is more than a house. Think about the ways you make your house a home. What are some things you would like to do?

- Making a home isn't the easiest job, but it is certainly the most rewarding.

- If your walls could talk, what would they say?

- If we aren't content with what we have, we will never be content with what we want.

- Spend time praying through your home. Go room to room and pray for the family members who spend time in that room. Ask God to bless the home and all the neighbors, strangers, friends, and relatives who enter the front door.

25

Be a Teaching Parent

Too often parents try to make life easier for their children. We complete a task because it's easier to just get it done than to patiently teach a child how to do it. Sometimes children complain so much and so loudly that we do it ourselves to save the arguments and hassles. There are many reasons why parents avoid becoming a teaching parent. They might start with the right intentions, but then life's demands cause them to go the way of convenience or quick fixes.

But if your heart's desire is to raise good, godly individuals who will grow up into fine, responsible adults, then they need to learn how to solve problems and to accomplish tasks without excuses.

Our society needs committed parents who are willing to spend the necessary time teaching the next generation the values and skills which will keep our country great. Yes, it takes more time and effort on our part to train children, but in the long run, the dividends will be tenfold for us and for them.

What a Teen Can Do

There's no greater calling than to be responsible parents to our children. Before the foundation of this earth, our children were planned just for us. We must believe and continue as best as we know how to raise and prepare our children for God's calling—wherever and whatever that might be.

Here is a list of some chores a young teen can do. Make these a part of their weekly responsibilities so that they learn a good work ethic and also discover the joy of a job well done. Choose a few from the following duties:

1. Make own bed
2. Put clothes back in the closet or proper dresser drawer
3. Put toys and games back in the proper areas
4. Water houseplants
5. Feed the dog, cat, or goldfish
6. Set the table
7. Clear the table
8. Empty wastebaskets
9. Carry out trash cans
10. Vacuum rugs and floors
11. Sweep and mop the kitchen floor
12. Iron own clothes and the family napkins and tablecloths
13. Polish silver, brass, and copper
14. Carry in wood for the fireplace
15. Vacuum the inside of the car
16. Wash the car

Train up a child in the way he should go,
and when he is old he will not turn from it.

PROVERBS 22:6

Use the following suggestions to help your children develop lifelong learning skills:

1. *Have family discussions.* Use dinnertime or other regular times to talk about current events, what happened at school or church, or to discuss ideas.

2. *Take family walks.* These are great times just to be together. Talk about whatever comes up. Often these walks bring up questions about flowers, waves, trees, and life.

3. *Go to the library.* At an early age have children get to know the library. With the Internet we often can find information that we might want to know about, but the library should feel like home to the youngsters.

4. *Make TV a learning tool.* Let the children learn that TV is more than just entertainment and cartoons. It is a valuable tool to stimulate your mind, see concerts, learn about nature, literature, and many social issues.

5. *Encourage your child to keep a journal.* Make sure your child knows that this is private unless they want to share the entries with you. This journal can include whatever they wish to enter (words, drawings, emotions, ideas, goals).

6. *Use a map or globe to show places mentioned in the news.* Discussing current events is a great way to teach history and geography. The world changes daily, and the children can be kept abreast of the issues by finding the event's origin on a map or globe.

7. *Visit museums.* Almost every midsized city has some kind of museum. If not, then a short drive will provide for good adventure. Family vacations can certainly include visits to such places.

8. *Listen to music together.* This is a great way for them to tell you about their music and for them to learn about yours. Learning about different kinds of music is certainly an eye-opener for all. Discuss what was enjoyable, interesting, or disappointing about each selection. Listening to a variety of music while in the car is a great way to break up the silence or boredom of long drives.

9. *Visit historical sites.* Start with the historical sites in your own

town. Many people don't really know about their own cities. Next, branch out to other sites. Vacations are a great time to learn about your various societies. It also develops curious minds.

10. *Tell each other stories.* They can be real or make-believe. Have one person begin by saying, "Once upon a time..." and then let others add on to the story.

11. *Read together.* Develop a routine where the family spends time reading together. When the children are young, Mom and Dad do the reading, but as the children grow older, they can be the narrator.

12. *Share your faith.* This can be a rich time in your family's life. The children can hear how faith has helped you and made a difference. Use this time to read from the Bible, sing songs, pray together, and ask questions.

13. *Make time for art.* Create an evening to draw together. The weekly activity can be a group mural or an individual activity. Provide all the materials. The family might explore a different medium each week: finger paints, poster paints, watercolors, clay, chalk. Bring in a guest who can teach some form of art.

14. *Perform family plays.* These are great evening activities. Turn off the TV and let your creative juices flow. Children love to dress up in vintage clothes, funny hats, and goofy slippers. Our plays were always structured around holidays, biblical stories, and current events.

15. *Ask open-ended questions.* Write down all kinds of questions that a family might want to ask. Write them on separate slips of paper and put them in a bowl. Have the family gather together. Pass the bowl around the group. Have each individual take one question and hold it until their turn comes about. You might ask these types of questions:

- What was your best vacation?
- Tell something about your grandmother.
- What was/is your favorite subject in school? Why?

- Who is your favorite Bible character? Why?
- What is your favorite season of the year? Why?
- Describe what you like about your brother/sister.

16. *Provide a computer for your child.* In today's age of technology it is important that your child be exposed to different kinds of software, research websites, word processing, emails, etc. If you can't afford a computer, check your local school or library to see if they offer public access. Often your local community college or center will have classes just for beginners.

17. *Have game night.* Family games are great for bringing together the family members. A lot of laughs, popcorn, and fruit drinks. Encourage the family to invite a guest if they wish.

How to Get Along with Your Child

As a parent, I can offer you many tips on parenting. But it is also important to find out what children have to say about the art of getting along. Here are some suggestions from students at Conestoga Valley Junior High. Pay attention. These are likely a few of the suggestions your own child would like to make.

- "Don't ask me to do something when I'm busy doing something else."
- "Try to put up with family members' bad moods because we all have them."
- "Listen carefully to me."
- "Listen before you yell."
- "Give your children some time when they can talk to you without any interruptions."
- "Even though our problems may seem ridiculous to you at times, don't tell us to forget them. Give us advice."
- "Lighten up a little."
- "Trust me with my own money."

- "Realize that I am my own person. I am not anything like my sister."
- "Remember, your kids try hard to please you."
- "Remember to count to 10…or 20."
- "Make sure you tell your kids how much you appreciate having them around."
- "Admit it when you're wrong."
- "Be honest with each other."

SIMPLE IDEAS

- Encourage teamwork. It's a lot more fun to work with someone else than by yourself.

- From time to time have your children write your shopping list for you.

- Teach your children how to write thank-you notes. No emails allowed.

- Help your children acquire a pen pal in a country that is of interest to them.

- Use a timer. Many children tense up during timed tests and may need to practice working under pressure.

- Put family weekend chores in a hat. The whole family works at each chore until it is completed.

- Let your children hear you pray for them. They will gradually come to know the wonderful Person you are talking to—the One who cares for them.

- The most powerful forms of praise are given in private, one-on-one.

- When your children are riding in the car on a trip, they can make up games to amuse themselves. One of the favorite games is: "I'm looking for…" The object can be anything—a red truck, a blue blouse, a pine tree. The first child to see the object gets to pick the next one.

- Here's an easy recipe for homemade finger paints: Mix ¼ cup cornstarch with 2 cups cold water. Bring to a boil. Let cool, then pour into paper or plastic cups and add food coloring.

26

Manners with a Fresh Approach

Nothing gives me greater satisfaction than to see my children and grandchildren using good manners. I believe it is a reflection of their upbringing. But this era of fast-food restaurants, instant communication, abbreviated email language, explicit song lyrics, and risqué fashions has made teaching manners all the more difficult.

Each family must decide how good manners are to be taught and exhibited. I love to go to the Southern states because for some reason the populace still believes in having good manners. When I visit there, I hear, "Yes, ma'am," "Miss Emilie," "Excuse me," "Please pass the tea." It's music to my ears.

When my grandchildren come for dinner, I announce to them that they will be dining in a very fine restaurant, and they must bring their best manners with them. Often in our haste to clean the house and polish the silver, parents are likely to forget that children's manners also need polishing from time to time.

Children with manners will feel more comfortable and confident in social situations. Often when we are out with the family, we have others give us a compliment on how polite and well-behaved the children are.

The kids love to hear these comments about themselves. They receive the blessings when others make favorable comments.

Keep these tips in mind as you teach young children about manners:

- *Work on one thing at a time.* Don't give too much information at once or the children will be overwhelmed and give up. Concentrate on one thing. Maybe go over telephone manners first, and then work on introducing a person to a guest the next time. Periodically review past teachings so the skill will not be forgotten.

- *Children will make mistakes.* Be patient with the students. They, like us, will periodically forget what has been taught, and they will forget proper behavior in certain situations. Use these mistakes as a learning situation. Don't correct the child in front of others—wait for a one-on-one situation so you can point out the proper response. The more tolerant, patient, and encouraging you are at these times, the more progress you'll see ultimately.

- *Catch your children doing good.* In our home we often use our "Caught being good" stickers. We hand these out when we catch our children doing something special when they haven't been asked to do so. These positive reinforcement moments are priceless. Too often we respond negatively when the children make a mistake. How about reacting positively when they do something good? If your child remembers the proper way to greet someone when being introduced, lean over and whisper, "That was great! I'm proud of you." You will probably see a big smile appear on your child's face.

The heart of all good manners is the
Golden Rule.
"Do unto others as you would
have them do unto you."

- *Know when to ask the right question.* When children don't respond in a proper way, try using a question to lead them to the right response. You might ask, "What's the first thing we do when we sit down to the table?" instead of saying, "You forgot to place your napkin in your lap." The question offers them an opportunity to respond. A criticism causes embarrassment and anger. Do this in a family situation, but with guests or when out in public, wait until you are alone with your child. When they respond properly you can respond with praise: "That's right. Good for you!" When teaching manners, we don't want our corrections to become like the sound of a dripping faucet. If we do, we will only confuse and discourage the learner. Children often learn by watching, not so much by talking.

- *Review guidelines before special events.* When you have an important or special event coming up, go over the skills and manners the children can exercise during the party, dinner, or visit to someone's home. Going over these guidelines early helps children draw up a game plan, have a review of what's expected of them, and minimize surprises. The children feel more at ease when they know what will happen.

- *Always accent the positive.* Bees respond to honey more than to vinegar. So do children! A good teacher leads by example and also gives good reasons why something is done a certain way. For example, when a child reaches for salt and pepper without asking, "Please pass the salt and pepper," you can say, "The reason we let other people pass things to us at the table is because reaching can cause spills and accidents." At the same time you can compliment them for helping the guests with their jackets and purses earlier. Always end on a positive note.

- *Be the example.* Children's eyes will give them examples of your manners. If you want to teach good manners, good manners must be important to you.

It's a real pleasure to be around well-behaved children. Teach your children how to behave properly in all situations.

SIMPLE IDEAS

Model manners and introduce your children to the basics.

- When giving a handshake, hold your hand out with your fingers together and your thumb up. Don't make a face if the other person squeezes too hard. Don't you squeeze too hard.

- Keep in mind four important manner phrases: please, thank you, excuse me, I'm sorry.

- It is never a good idea for a child to tell a caller he or she is home alone. Teach them to reply, "I'm sorry, they can't come to the phone right now. I'll be glad to take a message." You don't need to fib and say something like, "Oh, my mom is in the shower." It's best to be polite and calm.

- The heart of manners is always the same: showing kindness and respect for others.

- Do you know that smiling while on the telephone makes your voice sound friendlier? Put a sign next to your phone that says, "Smile."

- Practice saying, "After you." Let other people go through doors first or have the first choice. Your turn will come.

- Respect others' privacy, including that of your family members.

27

Inexpensive Activities and Outings

There is no substitute for the family's role in teaching and modeling the values and life goals that form the basis for decision making and for developing a personally fulfilling life. Today most of us struggle with the pressures of time and money, and family vacations and commercial entertainment are simply not options as much as we would like.

Let's return to a simpler way. Instead of driving each of four family members to a different activity, approach family recreation with creative flair and you will save time and money. It is not so much what is done, as much as how it is done that will nurture a family. In the years to come, few will remember what experiences cost or didn't cost. However, the memories of laughter and being together as a family will be vivid. The building and strengthening of a family is the greatest contribution to our society and to the future of our country.

1. *Adopt an older adult.* Go to a nursing home and find someone your family would like to adopt. Make periodic visits to this person, do favors for them, write them cards and letters, contact them by telephone.

2. *A kid-planned block party.* Have your children, along with others

165

in the neighborhood, design, produce, and conduct a block party for the families nearby. They can plan games, the menu, everything.

3. *Games tournament.* Games like volleyball, croquet, horseshoes, and badminton can be purchased for very little at garage sales or may be stuck in your garage, basement, or attic. Get them out and have a tournament.

4. *Three wishes.* Everyone in the family writes three things they would like to do that cost nothing and would involve the whole family. Put the wishes in a hat and draw for the one you will do first.

5. *Stargazing.* Books to assist your stargazing are available in the library or simple charts in most newspapers help to identify the major constellations. Find an open space as far away from city lights as possible. Lie down on your back and see how many stars and constellations you can identify. A flashlight with a strong beam would be helpful in pointing out locations for others to see.

6. *Campout at home.* Put up a tent or just roll out the sleeping bags in the backyard and spend the night out of the house. This is especially fun for younger children. The sleep out helps narrow the age gap between child and parent. A little fire, some good camp food, a few songs, and a story will make everyone believe they are camping in the wild.

7. *A family theme song.* Take a tune familiar to the whole family (hymns, current pop song, advertisement jingle) and, as a group, write new words for the song. Make the words positive and relate to your family, and you'll have your own family theme song.

8. *Visit work.* It would be very educational to spend an hour or two seeing the way each parent works and acts at work. Be sure not to make the visit too long so that young children with short attention spans can enjoy it. Introduce the children to your work friends, and let the family see some of the samples of the

finished product. A trip to a favorite lunch spot is sure to make the day a success.

9. *Bicycle trip.* Map out the route and scenic spots along the way. Take lunch and plenty of water, and switch leads so everyone learns basic rules.

10. *Weekend chores.* Write the chores on separate sheets of paper, place them in a hat, and draw for order of completion. The whole family works together.

11. *Cultural arts.* Every town has some often overlooked local groups. Review the available options and select an event to attend. Watching the local symphony, dance company, or theater group will introduce children to the performing arts.

12. *Feed the homeless at Thanksgiving.* Have the whole family assist a church or homeless shelter to prepare and feed those who are less fortunate. This is a great way to teach children and adults about gratitude and about being a servant. You may have your own Thanksgiving meal later, or you can donate your meal to the sponsoring organization.

13. *Storytelling.* The family can prepare a story for the evening, or they can tell about their favorite person and what they are like and why they admire them.

14. *Ecology project.* Take on ecology as a family project and start saving papers, aluminum cans, and other recyclable items. Or check for a conservation project near your home (erosion control, tree planting, stream cleaning, trash pick up, etc.). Select an activity where every member of the family can have an important role.

15. *Family T-shirt.* Make up a design for a family T-shirt. Let the whole family participate in the planning. The design for the shirt should be something that represents the strength of the family unit.

16. *Backyard obstacle course.* Set up a series of obstacles to go over, under, and around that will inspire physical fitness development.

Keep a record of individual times and the number of repetitions so that you can recognize progress.

17. *Family talent night.* Each of your family members can identify their talents, develop a show, and perform for a children's home or assisted living facility. This will be a great opportunity for the kids to be up front and to realize they have something to share with others.

18. *Neighborhood progressive dinner.* This will be a fun evening for your neighborhood families. Each family is assigned a course for the meal—appetizer, salad, soup, main course, dessert, etc. Members walk, ride bikes, or glide on skateboards from house to house.

19. *Role reversal.* Select a time when you and your children switch roles for a day. The children take charge of the parents' chores and responsibilities and the parents take on the children's roles and responsibilities. Take time afterward to discuss how it felt and any change of attitude inspired by the exercise.

20. *A restaurant at home.* Invite another family over and ahead of time prepare a restaurant-type meal. Different members of the family serve as waiters, cooks, or busboys. Print menus, play soft music for entertainment, and serve a several-course meal to add to the fun.

21. *Bike clinic.* As a family, take apart one of your bikes and put it back together again. Learn all you can about how the bike works. Start a regular bike maintenance program. The family members will take more pride in their bikes when they keep them clean and well maintained.

SIMPLE IDEAS

- Create a weekly time when your family gathers together to read the Bible and memorize a verse a week or month.

- Allow your kids to plan a dinner one night a week. Help them prepare the food if they are young, but as they grow older, let them do more of the cooking.

- Have a movie night for your children and some of their friends. Make popcorn and select a movie appropriate for the age group. Throw pillows down on the floor and let the kids get comfy.

- Plan a hike or a walk in an area that you don't get to often. Bring along Frisbees, footballs, or anything that suits your family for recreation. Bring along a picnic lunch to complete the afternoon.

- At the dinner table, have each member of the family share something they have learned that day or week. Discuss these new ideas or bits of information.

- Have your family sit in a circle for a praise night. Go around the circle and describe what you appreciate about each person. Have each one do the same. Spend a few moments closing in prayer to praise God—thanking Him for all that He does and is.

28

Woman to Woman

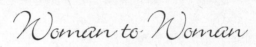

What is it about a good friend that makes her so special? Sometimes the simplest answer is the most profound. You like her. You feel better when she's around. You enjoy her company. Her presence refreshes you.

Some friendships are as comforting and comfortable as a well-worn pair of shoes. Others are full of excitement and adventure. The best ones are laced with laughter and softened with tears and strengthened with a spiritual bond. A friend is sensitive to the person you are. She listens both to the words you say and to the ones you cannot speak. She sees you, and she loves what she sees, and somehow you like yourself better when you're together.

> Life is either a daring adventure or nothing.
> To keep our faces toward change and
> behave like free spirits in the presence
> of fate is strength undefeatable.
>
> HELEN KELLER

Women today are on the move more than ever. We are wives, mothers, taxicab drivers, soccer moms, and so many other things. We often work out of our homes and sometimes even have a home business. While all of this is a blessing, it does not leave much time for friends. How do we keep close with our kindred spirits even when life is so full and busy?

You don't have to let friends become distant. Below are some stories of how friends make time to be friends:

- *Tea on the phone.* At least once a month Mary and Lisa prepare a cup of tea, get out a favorite scone or cookie, nestle up by the phone, and have a lengthy phone conversation sharing a favorite cup of tea. Each looks forward to the scheduled appointment with her friend.

- *Meet you halfway.* Two friends live three hours apart, and for ten years they have set aside one Saturday in November to be their day. They meet at a small outlet mall about half the distance for each of them. They get caught up on their shopping, but their main purpose is to catch up without husbands and children in tow and get renewed by each other's company.

- *Share a friendship ball.* Donna and I have been exchanging a small gift and note for years to keep our friendship strong. The gift must fit into a round, silver ball, and we must use the same box year after year. The sealing tape is so thick and heavy that the postage costs more than the gift. But several times a year, when I open that box and the friendship ball, I feel connected to my good friend.

- *Have a tea in a box.* Why not send your long-distance friend a tea in a box? Several of my friends have filled a box with all kinds of tea ingredients including tea, a teaspoon, a tea strainer, sugar cubes, linens, and even a vase for flowers. Add a few of your favorite scones and cookies and your friend is set for a special friendship tea.

- *Share a favorite television program together.* With unlimited long-distance phone service, you and your friends can do something separately but together. You can watch a favorite television show together—separately.

- *Share a devotional together.* Evelyn and Kathy share a weekly devotional together over the phone. During the week they study a certain passage of Scripture, and then on a set evening they call and share their thoughts. They report that this has been a great way to hold each other accountable in their faith.

- *Vacation together.* Have you ever thought of having seven families vacation together every summer? We have friends who do this! Each family takes a turn planning where they will vacation together the following year. They have prepared a set of guidelines for the host family to follow. This has been a success for ten years, and all families say it's the highlight of the year.

- *Have a phone chat.* Christy and Patti set aside 8:00 PM on Sundays to have a lengthy telephone chat. This is perfect with cell phones because weekend minutes are free. In four years, they have rarely missed an appointment.

A Friendship Story

My friendship with Maxine has lasted almost 50 years. We met in the eighth grade. My father was a minister in a small Nazarene church there. I invited Maxine to come to church with me one Sunday, and that one event started a friendship that has continued to this day. We both married men from a nearby Air Force base, located not far from the church. Our husbands, Merl and Ed, roomed together on the base and were also best friends. Maxine and I stood up for each other's wedding during our senior year of high school. Over the next few years we each had three children. All of them in consecutive order were born months and, in one instance, only three days apart. Though this was unplanned, it seemed ironic that we were still doing things together.

Later we were separated by many miles when my minister husband and I moved far away to Pennsylvania. Even then, Max and I kept in touch by letters and phone calls whenever possible.

Now, we are down to our retirement years in East Texas. Maxine and Ed moved within a mile and a half from us so that we could retire close to each other. What better ending than to repeat the beginning of our lives together?

Time has changed many things, but one thing that has grown dearer with the years has been our friendship. Even today, many people ask if we are sisters. Those silly schoolgirl years have matured into an enduring, unconditional friendship between the two of us. Maxine has always been the ideal friend who holds in her heart the intimate secrets of my life, as I do hers. What more could I ask than for someone to know me better than I know myself and still love me? I wouldn't trade the laughter and the tears for one moment without my best friends. There is no measure of wealth, no scale of greatness, no degree of success that could in any way replace a lifetime of friendship and blessing. God has given us this special gift of each other.

Mary Klink, Texas

Can miles truly separate us from friends?

RICHARD BACH

SIMPLE IDEAS

- Kindred spirits are not so scarce as I used to think. It's splendid to find out there are so many of them in the world. —Lucy Maud Montgomery

- Hold a true friend with both your hands. —Nigerian proverb

- Two are better than one, because they have a good return for their work; if one falls down, his friend can help him up. —The book of Ecclesiastes

- How would I answer the question, "What is a friend?"

- Friends give us fun and companionship and a sense of being connected to the world.

- This is what my special friendships have done for me...

- If I were to write a story of how a special friendship began, this is how it would go…

- Offer someone a ride to a meeting or other gathering. The gesture is usually appreciated, and the commute is a nice time to get to know each other better.

29

How to Overcome
Stress at Home

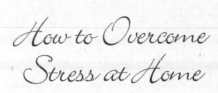

Ask yourself several questions to see if you are stressed-out at home. We all want to be calm and think that all is well with our organizational skills. Disorganization causes a lot of stress—the more organized you are, the less stress you will have in your life. So here goes. See how you do!

1. Do you have a certain place to store your unpaid bills until they need to be paid?
2. Do you have the habit of not finding your car keys or glasses easily?
3. Do you have a filing system to place all of your important papers, such as deeds, insurance policies, auto warranties, income tax records, health records, birth certificates, and escrow papers?
4. Is your car serviced on a regular basis?
5. Is your car fairly clean with a minimum of trash? Don't forget the trunk.

6. Do you hang up your clothes when you take them off or do you just leave them on the floor?

7. Is your yard regularly mowed and attractively maintained?

8. Do you save money each payday?

9. Do you spend less than you earn?

10. Do you have manageable credit card debt?

We could go on and on, but you get the idea that there are many areas in your life that can cause stress. If we don't take care of the little things in life, they will soon become the monsters of life.

Here is a common recipe for stress:

3 pounds of Hassles. Any of life's pressures or traumas will do.

5 cups of Hustle. These are common, everyday demands and can be supplied by any family member, neighbor, employer, children's club, church duty, or committee responsibility.

7 tablespoons of Hurrieds. You can pick them fresh off your schedule, expectations, and responsibilities.

Now stir them up and cook the mixture in the oven of life's trials. Hassled, Hustled, and Hurried—it's a fail-safe formula for a massive serving of stress. Serves one for 24 hours a day, 7 days a week, 52 weeks a year, unless spoiled by organization.

—Author unknown

The Perfect Woman

But how can we get organized? That is the million-dollar question. It seems as though today's woman is putting on a circus juggling act. She has to be superwoman. She not only has to attend all the extracurricular activities of the children, maintain involvement in church, school, and community activities, but she also has to be a good wife and mom.

A few years ago Dennis and Barbara Rainey provided an excellent description of what they call "the phantom wife."

Barbara's phantom is the perfect wife, mother, and friend, always loving, patient, understanding, and kind. She is well-organized, with a perfect balance between being disciplined and flexible. Her house is always neat and well decorated, and her children obey the first time, every time. She is serious yet lighthearted, submissive but not passive. She is energetic and never tired. She looks fresh and attractive at all times, whether in jeans and a sweater digging in the garden or in a silk dress and heels going to dinner. She never gets sick, lonely, or discouraged. And because her phantom is a Christian, Barbara sees her faithfully walking with God daily. This phantom prays regularly, studies diligently, and is not fearful or inhibited about sharing her faith or speaking the truth to someone who may be in error.[1]

While the Raineys' words may have you smile, they may also have opened your eyes to the false expectations our society has placed on women.

Next to God we are indebted to
women, first for life itself, and then
for making it worth having.

CHRISTIAN N. BOVEE

How many balls are we juggling in our lives? There are many expectations placed upon us—some real and some self-imposed. Sounds tough, doesn't it? No wonder we have balls dropping all around us. And with each drop we are caused more and more stress. We spend a lot of our energy worrying that the next ball to drop will be the one that hurts our family or ruins our futures. It's a lot of pressure.

Help Yourself Succeed

There is a recipe for beating stress. It's called organization. I'll bet you have a couple areas of your life that are well managed, but you have not been able to translate the skills you apply to that area to other parts of your life. Maybe you have never examined your formula for success to see if it would work across the board.

Here is a formula sure to beat stress and disorderly conduct:

- 1 quality period of time with God each day
- 1 list of carefully-thought-through long-term and short-term goals
- 1 list of priority activities to direct you toward achieving those goals
- 1 monthly calendar
- 1 weekly schedule book
- 1 pad of daily schedule forms
- 1 three-drawer file cabinet
- multicolored legal size file folders
- 1 small binder that contains basic organization forms to keep you on track

Involve the Family

Gather your family together and schedule a Saturday morning where all of you can come together and reorganize your things.

- *Invest in the proper tools.* You need the basic tools to assist you in being organized. Refer to the formula to beat stress for ideas.
- *Involve the whole family.* Learn to delegate jobs and responsibilities to other members of the family. My Bob takes care of all the repairs. When something is broken, he is Mr. Fix-It. Depending upon the ages of your children, you will need to tailor-make their chores. Don't do something yourself that another member of the family can do.
- *Keep master lists.* I've learned to use my three-ring binder, my 3 x 5 file cards, and journals to keep track of all our possessions and tasks. You may think you'll never forget that you loaned that CD to Brad or that video to Christine, but you will. Write it down and keep the list in a place where you cannot overlook it. Use the chart provided to keep track simply.
- *Continually reevaluate your system.* Nothing is written in con-

crete. See how other people do things, read a book to gather ideas, evaluate your own system. Change it when it's not working.

- *Use a lot of labels.* If containers, bins, drawers, and shelves aren't labeled, you and your family won't be able to spot where things go.

~ Items Loaned and Borrowed ~			
Month/Year Date	Item	Who	Returned

Make the Most of It

Realize that you are responsible for causing your own effects in life. Tackle the toughest, most challenging assignments in your life first, understanding that your gratification will come after you have made the effort to do the job.

Don't let days and weeks and months and years go by without a plan and without a sense of purpose in your life. Every minute of this life matters and is important. Even when you are relaxing or watching a sunset or sitting at the table with your kids—you are shaping a life that is precious. Make the most of it.

SIMPLE IDEAS

- Are you a morning person or a night person? Your efficiency may increase if you arrange your tasks as much as possible around the rhythms of your body.

- Assign jobs and responsibilities within the family.

- The key is to start now. If you have a call to make, start dialing. Have a letter to write? Start writing.

- Use small amounts of time (five to ten minutes) to your best advantage.

- Carefully plan the use of leisure time.

- Leave yourself some open-ended time for a spur-of-the-moment activity. Don't cram your appointment book full.

- To keep track of your credit cards, lay them out and photocopy them. All the info is on one page. Keep them in a safe and secure place.

- It's not what you get that makes you successful; it is what you are continuing to do with what you've got.

30

Creating Easy Family Meals

Here are some favorite recipes from my kitchen that you and your family can enjoy. They don't require a lot of muss or fuss and are sure to please. Simplifying mealtime can be one of the best time-savers.

Easy Meals to Start Your Day

from Emilie's Kitchen

Sunshine Shake

1 Serving

Wake up or reenergize with this tasty potassium-and-vitamin-C-rich drink!

Blend together until smooth in the blender:
  1 medium orange, peeled and cut in chunks
  1 medium banana, peeled
  ½ cup lowfat or nonfat plain yogurt or lowfat vanilla yogurt
  ¹⁄₁₆ teaspoon nutmeg
  ¹⁄₁₆ teaspoon cinnamon

1 serving (with lowfat vanilla yogurt): 271 calories, 10 grams protein, 61 grams carbohydrate, 2.5 grams fat (8 percent of calories), 5 grams dietary fiber

Minute Bran Muffins

Makes 10 to 12 large muffins

These go with everything! Serve warm or cold. I'm listing these as a great way to start your day, but these muffins are a great complement to lunches and dinners, and are a healthy midday snack.

Preheat oven to 350°. Grease muffin pan or line with muffin papers.

Cover ½ cup raisins with warm water for 5 minutes and then drain (optional).

Blend together and let stand for 5 minutes:
   ½ cup boiling water
   1 ½ cups unprocessed wheat bran

Blend together thoroughly with wire whisk in order given:
   1 egg
   ¼ to ⅓ cup honey
   1 cup buttermilk or sour milk
   bran mixture

Blend dry ingredients together in separate bowl:
   1½ cups whole wheat or whole wheat pastry flour
   1¼ teaspoons soda
   1 teaspoon salt
   ½ cup walnuts, chopped (optional)

Blend drained raisins into liquid ingredients, and then dry ingredients into liquid ingredients just until mixed. Do not overmix! Fill muffin cups almost full. Fill any empty cups halfway with water. Bake 20 to 25 minutes at 350°. Cool 5 to 10 minutes before removing from pan.

1 muffin (when 10 muffins made), (raisins/walnuts not included): 145 calories, 4.5 grams protein, 32 grams carbohydrate, 1.5 grams fat (11 percent of calories), 6 grams dietary fiber

Emilie's Deluxe Bran Muffins

Makes 12 large muffins

Follow recipe for Minute Bran Muffins using:
   1 cup chopped dates
   1 cup raisins
   1 cup chopped walnuts
   1 cup shredded coconut, unsweetened (optional)

1 muffin (coconut not included): 263 calories, 6 grams protein, 58 grams carbohydrate, 7.5 grams fat (26 percent of calories), 7 grams dietary fiber

from Emilie's Kitchen

Golden Waffles/Pancakes

4 to 6 servings—makes 3 to 4 large waffles or about 20 pancakes

This is a fabulous breakfast and even a great dinner.

Blend together dry ingredients:
 1½ cups whole wheat flour
 1½ cups stone-ground cornmeal
 1 tablespoon baking powder
 1 teaspoon salt

Mix into dry ingredients:
 4 eggs
 2½ cups buttermilk, as needed for consistency

Spray hot waffle iron or pancake griddle with cooking spray or add 1 tablespoon melted butter or oil to batter to prevent sticking. Use a measuring cup to pour batter onto the griddle or the waffle iron.

Variations:
- For lighter waffles or pancakes, separate the eggs, beat egg whites until stiff but not dry, and fold into batter last.
- Add chopped nuts to batter or sprinkle over top of each waffle just before closing waffle iron lid to bake. Pecans or sunflower seeds are good.
- Add 2 to 4 tablespoons melted butter or vegetable oil for a more delectable texture.

Serve with:
 Unsweetened applesauce and/or pure maple syrup or fresh strawberries
 Lowfat vanilla or plain yogurt

1 serving (when 6 servings made, added fat not included): 317 calories, 14.5 grams protein, 50 grams carbohydrate, 7 grams fat (20 percent of calories), 7.5 grams dietary fiber

Delicious Lunches or Dinners

from Emilie's Kitchen

Baked Parmesan Chicken

6 5.3-ounce servings

Preheat oven to 350°

Melt in baking pan at about 250°:
   ½ cup (1 stick) butter

Meanwhile, mix together in blender until small bread crumbs are formed:
   1 slice whole wheat bread or amount needed to make about 1 cup soft crumbs, not packed
   2 or 3 sprigs fresh parsley to make about ¼ cup minced
   ½ cup Parmesan cheese
   ⅛ teaspoon garlic powder
   ⅛ teaspoon salt

Remove skin and visible fat from chicken:
   2 pounds boneless chicken breast pieces

Remove melted butter from oven and coat chicken first with the butter, then with crumb mixture. Lay chicken in remaining butter in pan, top with any remaining crumb mixture, sprinkle with paprika if desired, and bake uncovered at 350° until tender, about 1 hour.

Baste chicken a couple times during baking. Cover with foil if coating starts to brown too much before chicken is tender.

1 serving: 491 calories, 52.5 grams protein, 5 grams carbohydrate, 26.5 grams fat (49 percent of calories), 0.5 grams dietary fiber

Reduced fat variation:
   • Reduce Parmesan cheese to 3 tablespoons.
   • Omit butter; bake in nonstick pan or pan coated with Pam spray.
   • Dip coated chicken pieces in nonfat milk, as needed, in place of melted butter.

1 serving: 344 calories, 51.5 grams protein, 6 grams carbohydrate, 10 grams fat (10 percent of calories), 0.5 gram dietary fiber

Serve with: brown rice or brown rice pilaf, green or yellow vegetable, tossed salad

from Emilie's Kitchen

Eggplant Parmigiana

6 servings

Beat 2 eggs lightly with a fork in a wide, shallow bowl. Place 1 cup stone-ground cornmeal in another wide, shallow bowl. Thinly slice 1 medium eggplant, unpeeled into ⅛"-thick slices.

Dip eggplant slices first in eggs, then in cornmeal.
Brown lightly in olive oil, as needed.
Drain slices well on paper towels.

While slices are browning assemble:
2 8-ounce cans tomato sauce
2 cups mozzarella cheese, grated
¼ cup grated Parmesan cheese
2 teaspoons sweet basil

Make 2 or 3 layers of the ingredients in a lightly greased 9 x 13 pan in this order:
eggplant slices
sauce
cheeses
sweet basil

Cover and bake at 350° for 20 minutes or until cheese melts and sauce is heated through.

1 serving (using ¼ cup oil): 346 calories, 18 grams protein, 26 grams carbohydrate, 19.5 grams fat (51 percent of calories), 4.5 grams dietary fiber

Serve with: green vegetable, carrots, cabbage, or tossed salad

from Emilie's Kitchen

Vegetable Lasagna

6 to 8 servings

Wash and then steam about 5 minutes until tender 1 bunch of fresh spinach and drain well. Chop and set aside.

Sauté in olive oil:
1 tablespoon olive oil
½ cup chopped onion
1 cup diced carrots

1 clove garlic, minced
1 cup mushrooms, sliced (add during the last minute or two)

Blend into sautéed vegetables:
2 cups tomato, pasta, or spaghetti sauce
2¼-ounce can sliced ripe olives, drained
1½ teaspoons oregano
1 teaspoon sweet basil

While sauce simmers, prepare:
6 cups thin unpeeled zucchini slices (about 3 medium)
½ cup grated sharp cheddar cheese
½ cup grated mozzarella cheese

Mix together in another container:
1 cup low-fat cottage cheese
2 eggs
¼ cup Parmesan cheese

Layer ingredients in lightly greased 9 x 13 pan as follows:
half the zucchini slices
half the cottage cheese mixture
half the spinach
half the grated cheeses
half the sauce mixture

Repeat the layers.
Cover and bake at 375° for 30 minutes.

Serve with: fresh pineapple spears, whole grain bread

1 serving (when 6 servings made): 309 calories, 19 grams protein, 18 grams carbohydrate, 12 grams fat (35 percent of calories), 13.5 grams dietary fiber

from Emilie's Kitchen

Almond Tuna Salad

2 servings

Mix together:
1 6.5-ounce can water-packed tuna, well drained
½ cup nonfat plain yogurt
2 tablespoons mayonnaise
2 teaspoons lemon juice

1 stalk celery, chopped
1 slice onion, chopped
⅓ cup chopped or slivered almonds

Arrange on each individual salad plate in the following order:
    leaf of green leafy lettuce
    2 cups broken leafy and iceberg lettuce
    1 tomato, cut almost through in wedges to form a tomato
      "flower"
    half the tuna almond mixture mounded in center of tomato
      "flower"

Sprinkle paprika on tuna mixture and place a ripe olive in the center.

Garnish with parsley sprigs.

Serve with: whole grain muffins or rolls, carrot sticks, and cucumber slices

1 serving: 403 calories, 35.5 grams protein, 13 grams carbohydrate, 23 grams fat (51 percent of calories), 0.5 gram dietary fiber

from Emilie's Kitchen

Savory Chili

8 servings

Soak 2 cups dry kidney beans overnight in 8 cups of water

Cover 1 block tofu (12 to 19 ounces) with water and freeze (optional).

Bring beans and water to a boil for 10 minutes, reduce heat, and simmer until tender, about 2 to 3 hours. Add more water, if needed.

Place frozen tofu, if used, in a colander and thaw under running water; squeeze out excess water and crumble.

Sauté in a little olive oil:
    1 onion, chopped
    2 cups sliced fresh mushrooms
    1 green pepper, chopped
    2 cloves garlic, minced

Add to beans when tender:
    2 15-ounce cans tomato pieces
    sautéed vegetables
    crumbled tofu (optional)

1 tablespoon chili powder
1½ teaspoons cumin powder
1 teaspoon salt, to taste

Simmer 30 minutes longer to blend flavors.

Serve with cornbread, carrot salad, or carrot and celery sticks

1 serving (oil not included): 251 calories, 17 grams protein, 40 grams carbohydrates, 3.5 grams fat (13 percent of calories), 8 grams dietary fiber

from Emilie's Kitchen

Split Pea Soup

4 servings

A family favorite, familiar to everyone. Surprisingly tasty—even without a ham bone!

Bring 1½ cups split peas (washed) in 6 cups of water to a boil for 3 minutes, reduce heat and simmer until peas are tender—45 to 60 minutes.

Add and continue to simmer until vegetables are tender, 15 to 20 minutes, adding more water as needed:
   ½ cup chopped onion
   2 fresh carrots, diced or sliced
   3 stalks celery, chopped
   1 to 2 teaspoons salt, to taste
   1 bay leaf

Remove bay leaf. Puree part or all of soup in blender, if desired. This will help to thicken the soup.

Serve with: vegetable salad or vegetable relish tray and whole wheat bread, whole grain bread toast, or minute bran muffins (see breakfast recipes)

Per 1½-cup serving: 290 calories, 19 grams protein, 52 grams carbohydrate, 1 gram fat (3 percent of calories), 10 grams dietary fiber

from Emilie's Kitchen

Golden Stuffed Potatoes

4 servings

A tasty alternative to butter-laden potatoes! These are a big hit when served to company. Serve with no extra butter at the table.

Wash and bake 3 baking-sized (8 ounces) potatoes at 400° until done, about 1 hour.

Meanwhile cut the following into 3" chunks: about 1 pound banana or yellow squash, seeds removed, to make 1¼ cups mashed cooked squash.

Place squash skin-side down in vegetable steamer over boiling water, cover, and steam until very tender, about 20 to 30 minutes. Add more water, if needed.

When squash is cooled off enough to handle (but still very warm), scoop squash from skin with a spoon into electric mixer bowl (if you have one—otherwise into regular mixing bowl).

When baked potatoes are cool enough to handle (but still hot), cut in half lengthwise and scoop potato with spoon into bowl with the squash.

Add:
   1 tablespoon soft butter
   1 teaspoon salt
   ⅜ to ½ teaspoon cumin powder, to taste

Blend until smooth with electric beaters or potato masher. Pile potato-squash mixture into potato shells. Garnish with paprika. Place in covered pan or casserole and return to oven to heat through.

Serve with: amandine green beans or green vegetable and apple coleslaw

1 serving: 113 calories, 2.5 grams protein, 19 grams carbohydrate, 3 grams fat (25 percent of calories), 4 grams dietary fiber

from Emilie's Kitchen

Lentil Rice Casserole

6 servings

Blend together in a casserole dish:
   3 cups chicken broth
   ¾ cup lentils, uncooked
   ½ cup brown rice, uncooked
   ¼ cup instant minced onion (or ¾ cup fresh chopped)
   ½ teaspoon sweet basil
   ¼ teaspoon oregano
   ¼ teaspoon thyme
   ¼ teaspoon garlic powder

Bake covered for 2 to 2½ hours at 300°

During the last 20 minutes of baking, top with ½ cup grated cheddar cheese (optional).

Just before serving, stir to blend in the melted cheese and garnish with a handful of minced fresh parsley.

Serve with: plain yogurt or barbecue sauce, green or yellow vegetable, tossed salad

1 serving without cheese: 155 calories, 9.5 grams protein, 29 grams carbohydrate, 0.5 grams fat (4 percent of calories), 3.5 grams dietary fiber

1 serving with cheese: 193 calories, 10.5 grams protein, 29 grams carbohydrate, 3.5 grams fat (17 percent of calories), 3.5 grams dietary fiber

SIMPLE IDEAS

Zip-top plastic bags are not just for food storage. They also can make other kitchen tasks easier and less messy. Here are some uses that make life simpler in the kitchen.

• Marinating meat and poultry: Put marinade ingredients in a large bag (you may need only half as much as usual). Seal bag, shake to mix ingredients, then add meat, press the air out of the bag, and reseal. Refrigerate, turning bag occasionally.

• Making deviled eggs: Put hard-cooked egg yolks and other ingredients into a zip-top bag and knead until blended and smooth. Press mixture into one corner of the bag, cut off the tip, then squeeze mixture into egg white halves.

- Coloring cookies: Put plain vanilla or sugar cookie dough in the bag. Add a few drops of food coloring, press out air, seal, and knead until the color is blended. (No dyed hands!)

- Freezing for fast thawing: Fill bags with ground meat. Place on countertop and press into a flat layer that fills the bag. Seal, label, and freeze.

OTHER IDEAS

- A two- to three-ounce portion of chicken, fish, or meat will look like a lot of food if you cut it into chunks or strips and pile it loosely on your plate.

- To slice flank steak, pork tenderloin, or boneless breast of chicken in your food processor, partially freeze the meat beforehand. It will cut into thin, even slices.

- Leftover orange, lemon, or lime rinds are great garbage disposal deodorizers.

Travel

> For everything there is a season,
> and a time for every matter
> under heaven.
>
> ECCLESIASTES 3:1 RSV

31

Gear Up for Vacation Time

∽

Vacation time, here I come. I want to read, swim, eat, and sightsee. If you are like me, you'd like to catch up on your rest and relaxation to overcome your tiredness. As you plan your vacation, do block out some time just to rest. The book of Psalms says, "Be still and know that I am God."

Economists and financial analysts are telling us that domestic travel is on the rise. So, even if you've planned to relax a little closer to home than usual, don't let your guard down. Taking the same precautions for a short trip that you would for a trip around the globe is a good idea. As with all areas of your life—preparation saves time and money and energy. And we like our energy, don't we?

Here are some time-saving hints to help you plan for that great getaway adventure. Consider these few tips to be a refresher of what you already know, and maybe there is a thing or two you haven't thought of.

- *Test your alarm system.* Make sure it's working properly.
- *Put your house lights on timers.* If you'll be gone more than a

few days, invest in ones that will turn the lights on and off at different times of the day.

- *Adjust the settings on your thermostat.* No use cooling or heating your home if you're going to be away. It also will save you money.

- *Turn off the water to your washing machine.* You don't want to come home to a busted hose and a flood.

- *Tell a good neighbor or friend where you're going.* It's always wise to give them your address/destination and the phone number of your final destination.

- *Ask a neighbor to set out and bring in the trash cans.* You want to give the impression that someone's at home.

- *Stop mail and newspaper delivery.* Or you can ask a neighbor to bring them in while you're gone.

- Use a travel checklist for your organizational needs and then make a copy for a family member or a neighbor.

Bon Voyage

Now that your home is secure, you can be on your way. One of the best tips for safety in unfamiliar territory is to blend in with the crowd. Tourists attract crime the way boy bands attract teenage girls. Check the maps before you leave your hotel room. Looking lost and reading maps in public mark you as a tourist and as a stranger to the area.

- *Conceal your camera.* Don't walk through crowds and down the city streets with your camera equipment and bags on display. Cameras have become so small they can easily be carried in a pocket or average tote bag. Also, don't flash expensive jewelry, watches, and the like. It's a sure way to be spotted by pickpockets and robbers.

- *Be cautious with your shoulder bag.* If you carry a shoulder bag, keep it close to your body. Try to arrange it so the end of the zipper closes toward the front...and rest your hand lightly on that area of the bag. It looks natural and can prevent a pickpocket from getting a hand into your bag.

Travel & Vacation Checklist

Destination: _____

_____

Airline: _____ **Flight #:** _____

Depart/Date & Time: _____

Arrival/Date & Time: _____

Airline: _____ **Flight #:** _____

Depart/Date & Time: _____

Arrival/Date & Time: _____

Airline: _____ **Flight #:** _____

Depart/Date & Time: _____

Arrival/Date & Time: _____

Accommodations: _____

   Address: _____

   Phone: _____

   Children: _____

_____

   Pets: _____

Deliveries to Be Stopped: _____

_____

Mail: _____

_____

Special Purchases for Trip: _____

_____

Recommended Activities: _____

_____

Recommended Restaurants: _____

_____

Notes: _____

_____

_____

_____

- *Stay on well-lit streets.* Keep to well-traveled streets…no back alleys or shortcuts.

- *Lock your car.* Always lock your car when parked, even if it's just a brief stop. Keep valuables out of sight, preferably locked in the trunk. Don't leave your maps and guidebooks visible on the seats. Put them in your glove compartment or conceal them under a seat.

- *Check for bank locations.* Check with your bank for branch locations in the city you are traveling to. If they don't have one there, ask about ATM locations. And you may also want to let your bank and credit card company know that you are traveling out of the area. Some companies will lock your credit card if they notice an unusual amount of activity in an area away from your billing address.

- *Check ATMs at police stations.* Many police departments now have ATMs available 24 hours in their lobby. It may cost an additional transaction fee, but you won't get much safer service if you have to get some cash after dark.

- *Relax and have fun.* Don't panic and don't obsess. Don't be afraid to talk to the locals; they usually know the best places to eat. Just take some common sense precautions and remember the most important tip of all…have a great time.

SIMPLE IDEAS

- For most travelers, it's best to carry no purse at all. It can be snatched by a swift bicyclist. Wear a money belt, and if you must take a purse, make it a fanny pack.

- Park with your car wheels turned sharply to the curb, to make towing difficult.

- Get a car alarm system to frighten off thieves with sirens, horns, and/or lights.

- Make a note of your traveler's check numbers and photocopy your passport identification pages, driver's license, and all credit cards you are taking with you. Give copies to a friend, and tuck other copies in your wallet and luggage.

- Keep airline tickets, extra traveler's checks, and other valuables in hotel safe-deposit box.

- If you use your home address on luggage tags, get tags that have a flap to conceal the information from casual observers.

- If you are traveling overseas, learn enough of your host country's language to be able to communicate your need for assistance.

- Check the routing of your baggage. Make sure the agent attaches the correct tags for your destination city.

- Leave for the airport early. Allow for car trouble and overcrowded street traffic.

- Keep a record of your vehicle identification number in a safe place.

- In case checked bags don't make it, pack carry-on bags with: medicines, toiletries, vitamins, extra eyeglasses, night clothes, underwear, shirt, folding umbrella, thin raincoat, and a miniature sewing kit. Keep jewelry, passport, and other documents, including prescriptions and essential medication, in your purse or briefcase.

32

Tips for Healthy Travel

⁓

When traveling by plane, you will face increased security, having to arrive two hours before plane departure, and the possibility of canceled flights and increased stress. But flying can still be a good, convenient, and healthy way to travel if you take care of yourself.

It is important to focus on your health and well being when traveling. The suggestions below offer some advice that may help you during your flight travels:

- *Stay hydrated.* Drink plenty of fluids, such as water or fruit juices. Limit caffeine and alcohol, which can cause dehydration.

- *Use both hands.* More and more travelers are carrying on luggage that is heavy. Use both hands when retrieving objects from the overhead compartment to avoid strains and sprains.

- *Keep your skin moist.* The airflow in airplanes tends to dry out your skin. Frequently apply moisturizing cream to your hands and face.

- *Relieve pressure in the ears.* Many travelers, particularly children, have difficulty with pain in their ears while flying. Try chewing gum, sucking on bite-sized candies, swallowing frequently, or yawning.

- *Avoid crossing your legs.* The slightest pressure on your legs will reduce the amount of blood circulation. Your body needs maximum blood flow in order to get adequate oxygen to your body.

- *Breathe slowly and deeply.* In order to remain relaxed, it's important to keep oxygen flowing into your lungs. If needed, adjust the knob overhead to get more airflow.

- *Stretch regularly.* You can always walk the aisles of the plane to help keep your muscles working. There are also simple exercises you can do while seated. Some are:

  o *Shoulder rolls.* Lift your shoulders upward and then move them in a circular fashion for about 30 seconds.

  o *Ankle twirls.* Lift and rotate your feet in a circle for several seconds.

  o *Foot pumps.* Keep your heels on the floor and lift your toes as high as possible for a few seconds and repeat several times.

  o *Finger and toe stretch.* Clench fingers (toes) inward and then stretch them outward. Repeat several times with hands and feet.

  o *Knee lifts.* Hold your knee with both hands and lift it toward your chest. Hold this stretch for 15 seconds and let your knee down. Repeat with other knee.

  o *Neck roll.* Drop your right ear toward your right shoulder and gently roll your head forward to the left side. Then roll your head in the same fashion toward the right side. Repeat several times.

  o *Hug stretch.* Bring your right hand over your left shoulder and your left hand behind your right elbow. Gently pull the elbow toward your body and hold for a few seconds. Do the same with your left elbow. Repeat several times.

33

Fast and Smart Packing

Bob and I travel a lot doing seminars and occasionally for our vacations, and we're always amazed at the amount of luggage people take on their trips. As experienced travelers, we are constantly evaluating how much to put into our suitcase. Even after all of our trips, we still take too much; however, we are down to one suitcase each and one carry-on tote bag. This is yet another time when less is best.

Below are some helpful hints to get you off to a good start:

- Start with a checklist of what you want to have with you on your trip and assemble everything on the top of your bed. This way you can better visualize what you are packing. You may decide to eliminate some things as you pack if you find there's too much for your suitcase. (If so, don't be tempted to go out and buy a larger suitcase.)

- Have a supply of white tissue paper to layer between garments for wrinkle reduction, and use plastic bags to hold shoes and cosmetics. Pack a few extra bags to carry home wet bathing suits and dirty laundry.

- Place shoes (except those you plan to wear the first day) and other heavy items in the suitcase first. Because wool fabrics resist creases and wrinkles better than other fabrics, they can also be put in or near the bottom of the bag.

- Pack those items you plan to wear on your first stop last so they'll be easy to find and wrinkles will be minimal. Pack the shoes you'll need first within easy reach along the sides of the suitcase. For balance, place one at each side.

- Make as few folds as possible. Roll jerseys and other lightweight knits, as well as underwear and nightclothes. After buttoning or fastening dresses, jackets, blouses, skirts, and heavy sweaters, fold them lengthwise, in thirds, turning back each side, including sleeves. If necessary—such as for a full-length dress—fold crosswise only at one point to fit the suitcase. Fold pants crosswise only once.

- A pair of shorts or sleeveless blouse may be laid out flat without folding.

- If packing more than one pair of pants, place one pair with the waist at one end of the suitcase, the next with the waist at the opposite end, and so forth.

- Stuff small things in other items to save space and help maintain the shape of larger pieces.

A man's life does not consist in the
abundance of his possessions.

LUKE 12:15 RSV

SIMPLE IDEAS

- Of all the natural fibers, wool requires the least care. Wrinkles will relax if you give the garment a little time and space to air. Don't hang or fold wool knits unless they're heavy or bulky. Roll them before storing or packing.

- To keep belt buckles and metal trim on bags from tarnishing, give them a coat of clear nail polish.

- The weight of the beads can pull and distort the shape of a beaded garment, such as a sweater or a dress. Fold and store flat instead of hanging.

- Repel moths the natural, sweet-scented way. Make a spice mixture of equal parts cinnamon, cloves, orris root, and black pepper. Tie a spoonful in a piece of gauze or fine net and place in drawers or tuck into pockets of the garment.

- Don't hang knits, including jerseys. Their natural tendency to stretch is increased by gravity, so they soon lose their shape. Instead, roll them up and tuck them in the corner of a chest of drawers, just as you would when packing for a trip. Fold heavy or bulky knits.

34

Preflight Checklists

There is nothing worse than getting halfway to the airport and realizing that you left your passport on the bedroom dresser. But a checklist can alleviate all the what-ifs and "oh, by the ways" that can drive you nuts.

The following list can help you cover the essentials while you're packing and before you leave for the airport. You don't need any added stress when you're heading out the door.

- *Driver's license and/or passport.* Security screening requires photo IDs. Special accommodations can be made if ID has been misplaced or stolen. Check with airport officials a few days ahead of time if they are lost.
- *Credit card(s).* Electronic ticketing makes it easier than ever to retrieve boarding passes at kiosks with a credit card. When I purchase or pay for things out of the United States, I get the best exchange rate from my credit card company.
- *Medical and health insurance cards.* An unplanned trip to a doctor

or hospital while away from home can be stressful. Carry these important cards with you in case of an emergency.

- *Wallet.* Never leave home without it. If traveling overseas, you might want to carry it in a fanny pack or in your front pocket.

- *Single dollars for bills and tips.* Save time so you don't have to wait for change.

- *Chargers for all portable devices.* Your PDAs and cell phones can't keep you in touch if the batteries aren't kept charged.

- *Cell phone.* To keep in touch with family, friends, and the office, be sure to leave home with a fully charged cell phone. Make sure you are up to date with all your essential contact information.

- *ICE.* Not the kind you put in drinks, but the listing under ICE, standing for "In Case of Emergency" kept in the phone directory of your cell phone. Emergency workers and paramedics are trained to look there when someone is injured or unconscious to learn whom to contact or what medications, special conditions, or drug sensitivity you may have.

- *Power adaptors/converters.* Not every locale has the same electrical voltage, cycles, or plug adapters as we do in the United States. Check the power requirements for the countries you will visit.

- *Business cards.* For business travel or meeting new friends, a business card is the best way to introduce yourself.

- *Comfortable shoes.* Be sure to wear comfortable shoes while traveling. In some airports you have to do a lot of walking from one terminal to another.

- *Wrinkle-resistant clothing.* Maintenance-free clothing is the choice of the day—minimum ironing needed. Leave the linens at home.

- *Medications.* Always pack in a carry-on bag in case the airline misplaces your luggage.

- *Toiletries.* Having them with you will save time and money.

- *Reading material.* Relax during your flight with your favorite book or magazine.
- *Bottled water.* Air travel is very dehydrating. Take along a few bottles of water.
- *Hotel and car confirmation.* Take along your confirmation copies for reservations. It will minimize delays at the ticket counters.
- *Flight itinerary, airline tickets, and confirmations.* Because of electronic ticketing, it's easy to forget flight information. Print a copy of your itinerary before leaving home in case the airline has misplaced your confirmation.

He who every morning plans the
transactions of the day and follows
out that plan carries a thread that will
guide him through the labyrinth of the
most busy life....But where no plan
is laid, where the disposal of time is
surrendered merely to the chance of
incidents, chaos will soon reign.

VICTOR HUGO

SIMPLE IDEAS

- Create a list of things you want to do or see on the trip you are about to take.
- Consider keeping a travel journal while you are on your trip. Take time to record your experiences and your thoughts while away from home.
- If you are traveling with your spouse or a good friend, plan a special meal or adventure ahead of time. Look online or ask a travel agent and choose something that will be a real treat like a spa treatment, a boat ride, or an exclusive tour.
- When traveling long distances, make a list of the things you would like to

do en route. A plane ride to Europe will take hours and hours. Catch up on your letter writing, journaling, goal setting, whatever sounds right for the flight.

• You can have your own personal sound track for your travel experience. Whether you have an iPod or a CD collection, decide what music you would like to play during your travel and while you are at your destination.

• Research the place you are going. Take a printout or page of notes that has some key points of interest listed. Maybe list some little known facts about the area as well. Recreation can be educational as well as fun.

Notes

Chapter 16

1. Patrick M. Morley, *The Man in the Mirror* (Brentwood, TN: Wolgemuth & Hyatt, 1989), pp. 144-45.

Chapter 29

1. Dennis and Barbara Rainey, *Building Your Mate's Self-Esteem* (Loveland, CA: Group Publishing, Inc., 2004), p. 35.

500 Handy Hints for Every Husband
by Bob Barnes

Bob Barnes (*15-Minutes Alone with God for Men,* more than 180,000 copies sold) reaches out to husbands with time-tested, work-saving tips. In short chapters he presents helpful hints along with practical suggestions for implementing them. Bob encourages men to take an active role in home and life management. They'll discover how to save time and energy by...

- becoming more organized
- doing projects more efficiently
- implementing money management principles
- keeping equipment and vehicles properly maintained
- using goals to achieve long-term success

In the process of sharing proven ways to make life easier, Bob draws on his own experiences as a happily married husband to highlight ways men can improve their marriages through thoughtfulness, communication, and strength.

Harvest House Books
by Bob & Emilie Barnes

Bob Barnes

15 Minutes Alone
with God for Men

500 Handy Hints for Every
Husband

Men Under Construction

Minute Meditations for Men

What Makes a Man
Feel Loved

Bob & Emilie Barnes

15-Minute Devotions
for Couples

101 Ways to Love Your
Grandkids

Abundance of the Heart

A Little Book of Manners
for Boys

Minute Meditations
for Couples

Emilie Barnes

The 15-Minute Organizer

15 Minutes Alone with God

15 Minutes of Peace
with God

15 Minutes with God
for Grandma

Cleaning Up the Clutter

Emilie's Creative
Home Organizer

Everything I Know
I Learned in My Garden

Everything I Know
I Learned over Tea

Friendship Teas to Go

A Grandma
Is a Gift from God

Heal My Heart, Lord

Home Warming

I Need Your Strength, Lord

If Teacups Could Talk

An Invitation to Tea

Join Me for Tea

Keep It Simple
for Busy Women

Let's Have a Tea Party!

A Little Book of Manners

Minute Meditations
for Busy Moms

Minute Meditations for Healing
and Hope

Minute Meditations
for Women

More Faith in My Day

More Hours in My Day

Quiet Moments for
a Busy Mom's Soul

A Quiet Refuge

Safe in the Father's Hands

Simple Secrets to
a Beautiful Home

Strength for Today,
Bright Hope for Tomorrow

A Tea to Comfort Your Soul

The Twelve Teas®
of Celebration

The Twelve Teas®
of Christmas

The Twelve Teas®
of Friendship